P9-CZV-625

WITH CONTEMPORARY GRADUATION SPEECHES that dissect the world as it is and imagine what it could be, *The World Is Waiting for You* brings forth eighteen courageous figures who have dared to transform the podium into a pulpit for championing peace, justice, protest, and a better world.

"The voices of conformity speak so loudly. Don't listen to them," acclaimed author and award-winning journalist Anna Quindlen cautioned graduates of Grinnell College. Jazz virtuoso and educator Wynton Marsalis advised new Connecticut College alums not to worry about being on time, but rather to be *in* time—because "time is actually your friend. He don't come back because he never goes away." And renowned physician and humanitarian Paul Farmer revealed at the University of Delaware his remarkable discovery—the new disease Empathy Deficit Disorder—and assured the commencers it could be cured.

The prescient, fiery feminism of Gloria Steinem sits parallel to that of celebrated writer Ursula K. Le Guin, who asks, "What if I talked like a woman right here in public?" Nobelist and novelist Toni Morrison sagaciously ponders how people centuries from now will perceive our current times, and Pulitzer Prize winner Barbara Kingsolver implores us always to act and speak the truth.

The World Is Waiting for You speaks to anyone who might take to heart the advice of Planned Parenthood president Cecile Richards—"life as an activist, troublemaker, or agitator is a tremendous option and one I highly recommend"—and is the perfect gift for all who are ready to move their tassels to the left.

THE WORLD IS
WAITING FOR YOU

THE WORLD IS WAITING FOR YOU

Graduation Speeches to Live By from Activists, Writers, and Visionaries

Edited by

TARA GROVE and ISABEL OSTRER

THE NEW PRESS

NEW YORK
LONDON

The publisher has made every effort to contact all rights holders of reprinted material in *The World Is Waiting for You*. If notified, the publisher will be pleased to rectify any omission in future editions.

© 2015 by The New Press
All rights reserved.
No part of this book may be reproduced, in any form, without written permission from the publisher.

Requests for permission to reproduce selections from this book should be mailed to:
Permissions Department, The New Press, 120 Wall Street, 31st floor,
New York, NY 10005.

The publisher is grateful for permission to reprint the following copyrighted material:

"Listen to the Mustn'ts" from *Where the Sidewalk Ends* by Shel Silverstein. Copyright © 1974 Evil Eye Music, Inc. Reprinted by permission of the Estate of Shel Silverstein and HarperCollins Publishers.

"On Angels" excerpt from *The Collected Poems: 1931–1987* by Czeslaw Milosz. Copyright © 1988 by Czeslaw Milosz Royalties, Inc. Reprinted by permission of HarperCollins Publishers.

The lines from "Natural Resources." Copyright © 2002 by Adrienne Rich. Copyright © 1978 by W.W. Norton & Company, Inc., from *The Fact of a Doorframe: Selected Poems, 1950–2001* by Adrienne Rich. Used by permission of W.W. Norton & Company, Inc.

The lines from "Columbia" from *The Collected Poems of Langston Hughes* by Langston Hughes, edited by Arnold Rampersad with David Roessel, Associate Editor, copyright © 1994 by the Estate of Langston Hughes. Used by permission of Alfred A. Knopf, an imprint of the Knopf Doubleday Publishing Group, a division of Random House LLC, and by permission of Harold Ober Associates. All rights reserved.

Excerpt from "Once" from *Her Blue Body Everything We Know: Earthling Poems, 1965–1990 Complete* by Alice Walker. Copyright © 1991 by Alice Walker. Reprinted by permission of Houghton Mifflin Harcourt Publishing Company. All rights reserved.

Published in the United States by The New Press, New York, 2015
Distributed by Perseus Distribution

ISBN 978-1-62097-090-4 (hc) / ISBN 978-1-62097-091-1 (e-book)
CIP data is available

The New Press publishes books that promote and enrich public discussion and understanding of the issues vital to our democracy and to a more equitable world. These books are made possible by the enthusiasm of our readers; the support of a committed group of donors, large and small; the collaboration of our many partners in the independent media and the not-for-profit sector; booksellers, who often hand-sell New Press books; librarians; and above all by our authors.

www.thenewpress.com

Book design and composition by Bookbright Media
Printed in the United States of America

2 4 6 8 10 9 7 5 3 1

CONTENTS

THE WORLD IS
WAITING FOR YOU

Learn Not to Listen

Anna Quindlen

GRINNELL COLLEGE, 2011

THE MORE I THOUGHT about speaking to all of you today, the more I realized that the prevailing opinion is that my speech should be an extended apology. On behalf of the entire country, I think I was expected to say I was sorry that the economy had tanked during your college years, that the job market was looking lean, that the housing market had become uncertain—in other words, that we who came before you were handing off an unmitigated disaster. I'm not going to do that. I just can't. I'm not going to say that I'm sorry for any of you, because I'm not. Because I think, perhaps, more than any college graduates in recent memory, you have an unparalleled opportunity to remake this country so that it is stronger, smarter, and makes a whole lot more sense.

When American generations past felt dissatisfaction with our prevailing culture, with corporations estranged from both line workers and consumers, with politics held prisoner by polls and personal ambition, they had to fight a comfortable and deeply entrenched status quo. During the peace movement, the civil rights movement, and the second-wave feminist movement in the 1960s there was tremendous push back from millions of average Americans who believed that world dominance, military might, segregation, and old, familiar gender roles worked just fine. They didn't want anyone blowing up the old ways.

You don't have to worry about that. The old ways have blown up all by themselves, fallen under the weight of a system that was a Potemkin village of alleged prosperity and progress based on easy credit and crazed consumerism. A financial system in which it was possible to become rich and powerful while investing and trading in nothing at all. An information system paralyzed and sabotaged by the technology that was outstripping it. A political system for which too many held open contempt. A consumer culture making things that didn't last and that people didn't really need. What happens to a country that has developed the peculiar habit of shopping for recreation when it runs out of money? Well, it can either screech to a halt, or it can discover that its priorities need to be recalibrated and that "stuff" is not salvation.

The voices of conformity speak so loudly. Don't listen to them.

It's as though America was a house, and at a certain point the roof was so leaky, the walls so bowed, the termites so widespread that it began to crumble. Now don't misunderstand me; the bedrock is still there—the bedrock which too often we honor in the breech, but which we honor just the same. The bedrock of a free and fair society based on the constant and open exchange of ideas. But it would be a tragedy and a lost opportunity if all of you rebuilt and constructed a house that looked like what we had before—tried to build the same old house, which we now know was in large part a house of cards. Your parents, proudly here today, and their parents before them, perhaps proudly here today, understood a simple equation for success: your children would do better than you had. Ditch digger, to cop, to lawyer, to judge—that's how I learned it as an Irish Catholic kid growing up. We're now supposed to apologize to you because it seems that that's no longer how it works, that you won't inherit the SUV, which was way too big, or the McMansion that was way too big, or the corner office that was way too big. That you will not do better. But I suggest that this is a moment to consider what "doing better" really means.

If you are part of the first generation of Americans who genuinely see race and ethnicity as attributes, not stereotypes, will you not have done better than we did? If you are part of the first generation of Americans with a clear understanding that gay men and lesbians are entitled to be full citizens of this country with all its rights, will you not have done better than we did? If you are part of the first generation of Americans who assume women merit full equality instead of grudging acceptance, will you not have done better than we did? And on a more personal level, if you are part of the generation that ditches the eighty-hour workweek and returns to a sane investment in your professional life, the first generation in which young women no longer agonize over how to balance work and family, and young men stop thinking they will balance work and family by getting married, won't you have done better than we did?

Believe me when I tell you that we made a grave error in thinking doing better is mathematical, a matter of the number at the bottom of your tax return. At the end of their lives, people assess how they've done not in terms of their income but in terms of their spirit, and I beg you to do the same, even if those who came before sometimes failed to do so. And I beg you not to let fear define you. I have enough of a memory of this day of my own to know that at some level it is preposterous to say that right now. You should be afraid: of leaving what you know, of seeking what you want, of taking the wrong path, of not finding the path at all but simply muddling along. Your friends are going in one direction, you in another. From this safe and beautiful place, you pass through an estuary to the great ocean, and sometimes the current out there is harsh and the riptides are rough, and you will be afraid. But you have to learn to put the fear aside, or at least to refuse to allow it to rule you, because it's fear that tamps down our authentic selves, turns us into some patchwork collection of affectations and expectations, mores and mannerisms—some treadmill set to the prevailing speed of universal acceptability, the tyranny of homogeny, whether the homogeny of that straight world of the suits, or the spiky world of the avant-garde.

The voices of conformity speak so loudly. Don't listen to them. People are going to tell you what you ought to think and how you ought to feel. They will tell you what to read and how to live. They will urge you to take jobs they loathe themselves and to follow safe paths that they themselves find tedious. Don't do it. Only a principled refusal to be terrorized by these stingy standards will save you from a Frankenstein life made up of others' expectations grafted together into a poor semblance of existence. You can't afford to do that. It's what has poisoned our culture, our community, and our national character. No one ever does the right thing from fear, and so many of the wrong things are done in its shadow. Homophobia, sexism, religious bigotry, xenophobia—they're all bricks in a wall that divides us, bricks cast of the clay of fear, fear of that which is different or unknown. Our political atmosphere has been so dispiriting because so many of our leaders are leaders in name only. They're terrorized by polls and focus groups, by the need to be all things to all people, which means they wind up being nothing at all. They're afraid—to be bold, to be decisive, to be inventive. If they were, they might lose. As it is, they have often lost their way. Our workplaces are full of fear; fear of innovation, fear of difference. The most widely used cliché in management today is to "think outside the box." The box isn't just stale custom, it's terrified paralysis. If at work you ever find yourself uttering the sentence "We've always done it that way," I urge you to wash your own mouth out with soap and start fresh.

Too often our public discourse fears real engagement. It pitches itself at the lowest possible level, always preaching to the choir so that no one will be angry, which usually means that no one will be interested. What is the point of free speech if we're always afraid to speak freely? Not long ago I asked a professor of religion what she did to suit the comfort level of the diverse group of students in her class. "It is not my job to make people comfortable," she replied. "It is my job to educate them." I almost stood up and cheered. If we fear competing viewpoints, if we fail to state the unpopular, or to allow the unpopular or even the unacceptable to be heard because of some sense of plain-vanilla civility, it's not civility at all. It's the denigration of human capacity for thought, the suggestion that we are fragile flowers incapable of disagreement, argument, or civil intellectual combat. Open your mouths. Speak your piece. Fear not.

Believe me, as the mother of three college graduates, I can say unequivocally that we, your parents, have been paralyzed by fear as well. When you were first born, each of you, our great glory was in thinking you were absolutely distinct from every baby who had ever been born. You were a miracle of singularity and we knew it in every fiber. You shouted "Dog." You lurched across the playground. You put a scrawl of red paint next to a squiggle of green and we put it on the fridge and said, "Oh my God, Oh my God! You are a painter, a poet, a prodigy, a genius." But we're only human, and being a parent is a very difficult job. And over the years, we sometimes learned to want for you things that you did not necessarily want for yourself. We learned to want the lead in the play, the editorship of the paper, the lucrative job offer, the straight and narrow path that sometimes leads absolutely nowhere. We sometimes learned to fear your differences, not to celebrate them. Sometimes we were convinced conformity would make life better, or at least easier, for you. Sometimes we had a very hard time figuring out where we ended and you began. Guide us back to where we started. Help us not to make mistakes out of fear disguised as love. Learn not to listen to us when we are wrong, because sometimes we are. We have gone wrong in the stewardship of this nation and this planet. We have sometimes gone wrong in the management of our own lives. So I urge you today to sometimes ignore your elders, much as you love them, and to begin to say "no" to the Greek chorus that thinks it knows the parameters of a good life when all it knows is some one-size-fits-all version of human experience.

Fear not. You can do this. Your generation should be the model for my generation because you totally rock. You're more philanthropic, more tolerant, more balanced and open-minded than any in living history. You have shown us the way; don't let us talk you out of that. Think back. Think back to first grade when you could still hear the sound of your own voice in your head, when you were too young, too unformed, too fantastic to understand that you were supposed to take on the protective coloration of the expectations of those around you, when you were absolutely, certainly, unapologetically yourself, when you were not afraid of anything. You are well qualified to be and to create the next big thing for this nation because you leave here today with the most essential educational credential any twenty-first-century human being can have. During our lifetime, there has been a trend in colleges and universities toward creeping preprofessional-ism. Parents who are paying a fortune for tuition asked, "What are you going to do with it?" And too often, institutions responded by creating programs and majors that were perilously close to

How will your audacious and authentic new world work?

technical school. Here was the problem with that: necessary skills have shifted so quickly during our lifetime that technical skills were overridden by technology. What of those people who once learned to repair typewriters, who were keypunch operators, or even who serviced landline phones? They're becoming obsolete. In a culture in which knowledge is moving at the speed of sound, there is nothing more valuable than a degree from a first-rate liberal arts college, and that is what you will get here today.

One estimate is that the average American will have seven to ten jobs during her lifetime. If you can bring critical thinking—which is the basis of all you've learned here—to the table, you will be ready for work no matter what that work may be. We need that critical thinking at this moment. We need you to do it for us. If you have bright ideas about how to restore confidence in Wall Street, teach kids with disabilities, serve customers and clients and patients, get books into the hands of readers, or run schools that work, we are waiting breathlessly to hear them. We need all that and so much more. We need you to make this a fairer place, a more unified nation, a country that wipes out the bright lines that have created an apartheid, an apartheid too long denied. I know you hate to hear your parents say it when they're driving, but we are lost.

You owe this country your best efforts. You're lucky people. Many in this country will never get the kind of education you earned here. You stand in the place of others, past and present, as do I. I stand here today in place of—in tribute to—generations of women denied the right to the pen and the podium. Some of you are here in lieu of parents or grandparents who couldn't afford college, much less a college like this one. Being the lucky one confers great responsibility and even moral obligation. But it's not simply the obligation to live an examined life, to embrace each moment as though it might be the last. It's also to live each moment as though it might be the first. To throw your arms wide to the new, the unexplored, even to that of which you may be afraid. Don't cave to the status quo. Don't trade happiness for deferred gratification. Don't give up adventure for safety and security. The safe is the enemy of the satisfying. Deferred gratification has a way of being deferred forever. And the status quo, "business-as-usual," "the-way-things-have-always-been-done" has completely failed us. The last few years have made that eminently clear. How will your audacious and authentic new world work?

I don't know. Helpful, right? Except that "I don't know" is one of the most exciting sentences in the English language, because in the right hands it suggests not ignorance but discovery. It's the beginning of news reporting, medical research, stage preparation, business creation, legislation. I don't know. I don't know the answer to so many questions. Can Twitter ever be more than dopey haiku? Can the government ever really see beyond the bombastic fog that hangs over Washington? Can family life ever really be egalitarian, and prejudice ever become a distant artifact? Can we ever value the wealth of our spirit more than the size of our salaries? You can help answer those questions if you dare. Be brave, for your own sake and the sake of the rest of us. I know that sounds hard. But I can offer you some simple guidance from Henry James, the most complex and cerebral of men, who once wrote, "Three things in human life are important. The first is to be kind. The second is to be kind. And the third is to be kind." We've let kindness slip away in our culture, too, trading it for candor, which was not an even trade. Bring kindness back to our society.

With that old house in ruins and the new one still to be built, you are the people who have to have the ability, the audacity, the ideals to answer these questions and so many more. Samuel Beckett once said, "To find a form that accommodates the mess, that is the task of the artist now." The mess, the mess! That's finally what you are leaving with today—the mess! I won't apologize for that. Instead I want you to see it for what it is: an engraved invitation to transformation. Certainty is dead. Long live the flying leap. Take it. Use it. Bring it.

Be In Time

Wynton Marsalis

CONNECTICUT COLLEGE, 2001

You know, I never write a speech, because I feel that when you write something, you go long. But for this one, I wrote one, and if it goes long, I might just stop in the middle of it and start playing.

As you now sit in full bloom of youth, ingest the sweetness of this communal moment in celebration of your academic achievement. I want you all to bathe in this moment as if it were the noonday sun, which as you can see is not going to come out today. Look around at family and friends and savor what you all have accomplished. All, bask in the afterglow of good feeling as this day wears on and you end up sloshing through today's and tonight's and, in some exceptionally festive cases, next week's parties. Get as close to your freshly educated feelings and thoughts as you can stand to be without overdosing on your own magnificence. Lord, have mercy. Feel the full weight and power of your presence and enjoy the respect due one who has survived this four-year baptism by book.

But before you remove your cap and your gown today, I want you to go inside yourself and reflect on who you are and want to be in the world out here: big, chaotic, and not-giving-a-damn world who is no respecter of people large or small. Take stock of your graduation day clichés: "You will change the world with the incorruptible strength of your personal integrity, your unquenchable thirst for justice, your unwavering courage in the face of an uninformed public duped by lying leaders and an even more lying media." Savor these last sublime moments of parents financing your rebellion against them. Savor this. Remember this day, May 26, 2001, and remember how you're going to combat world hunger, desegregate the schools, attack commercialism, sexism, fascism, racism, and every other kind of "ism," because there's a bunch of "isms" that haven't been found yet. Remember that you're going to get rich, be famous, be respected in your field, find the perfect spouse, get a great job, and have wonderfully well-behaved and mannerly children. Brothers and Sisters, revel in the last days of babyhood. I look out and I can even see without the sun shining down on us that all of you have a shine, a glow; you possess the eternal optimism of the untried, the untested, the inexperienced, the unimpressed. Check yourself out, because it's a beautiful thing.

In full bloom of youth and life, take stock of time and the passing of time.

And someday soon—maybe today—someone who you don't know will ask you, "Where did you go to school? When did you finish?" And you will smile and say, "Connecticut College '01," and they will smile and say, "Wow! You're so young," and you'll smile, too.

And you'll go on from this blissful time, so pregnant with possibility, armed with a diploma, into the unruly, vulgar mass of competition, political intrigue, backstabbing, and street-level hustle known as the workforce.

You'll get the perfect job and the worst job, you will be promoted and you will be fired (never justified, never your fault) over the dumbest thing. You'll become rich and impoverished; your heart will sprout wings and it will cry; you will marry and you're going to divorce. You will have children or not. You will experience unspeakable joy and tragedy beyond tears.

Yes, Brothers and Sisters, someone will come up to you and ask you, "Where did you go to school and when did you graduate?" and you will say, "Connecticut College

'o1," and they will say, "Hmm! You don't look that old,"
and you will smile and reply, "Thank you."

But now, many of us will no longer shine and glow
with youthful optimism to the point of arrogance. Oh no,
many of us will bend our integrity to the times or the
situation. Many of us will thirst for justice and equality
only when our own throats are parched; many of us will
lose our sense of outrage as "ism" after "ism" is justified through repetition, redefinition, and then dismissal.
After all, we have a lot to protect: our jobs, our kids, our
homes, our standing in the community, our very fundamental way of living. But still there will be those blood-
hounds amongst us that never lose the scent of this day.
I can look out and point you all out, almost; they're going to pursue and pursue and pursue and they're going
to find. There will be those shining individuals that remember May 26, 2001, and the promises born of youthful
naiveté. They will stand firm in the batter's box—we're
talking about baseball, and Mr. Robinson is here—
left- or right-handed, still swinging for the fences though
life has thrown curve after curve after curve for strike
after strike after unhittable strike. And further on we all
shall go: those who strike out and those who strike.

Before removing your cap and gown today, I want you
all to look again upon your parents and grandparents and
your stepparents. I want you to look real close and recognize yourself in them. And you know what? If you really

don't see it because you're too lost in yourself, I want you to look a little closer or step a little further away. In full bloom of youth and life, take stock of time and the passing of time. And as you are promoted or demoted; as you purchase cars and computers and homes and trinkets and pay mortgages and alimony and child support, or not; as you skillfully scale the slippery slopes of success or fail as you gossip and backstab, and connive or remain stoically silent and advise; as you rush life away to get ahead or lazily slump and fall far behind—take stock of time.

You will be told that "Time is your greatest enemy, time is your greatest possession," "Hey, you better be careful with time because time don't come back," "Time flies," "Time is of the essence," "Don't waste time," "You must control your time," and, above all else, "Be on time." Well, friends, in the words of the great Louisiana jazz trumpet man Enute Johnson, "Son, don't worry about being on time, be in time." Because when you are "in" time, you can accept and experience a much larger slice of life as it unfolds. Instead of imposing your will on every situation, you focus on including everyone else, and just that little adjustment of attitude gives you the space to understand where and who you are.

You see, time is actually your friend. He don't come back because he never goes away. And you will go on. And you will see your kids graduate or not, and your candidate will win or not or get cheated even; sometimes that happens, and you will gain too much weight or you'll lose some; your husband will or won't get caught; your kids will elate or disappoint you; you will stay or move to Florida; and you will defend a corruption (to protect your earnings, of course) with philosophy, prose, and politics, and your kids will not agree, and you will blame it on their youth. You will see them graduate or not and some other too-long speaker will attempt to inspire your kids to embrace life with some set of principles or laws or rules that will or won't work and you will look at your kids and grandkids and assess this very moment that we're in right now as an achievement once again in your life. And they in the full bloom of youth will look past you to their friends and their future. And you will finance their rebellion against you.

Will you, when your kids and grandkids sit here, will you be still in the full bloom of youth? Will you be still steadfast in your integrity, bubbling and seething with anger over the "isms" that need to be confronted, arrogant and unimpressed by things large and small? Will you be on the firing line with the same zeal you possess right here today? Or will you be broken by the unceasing pressure of the crass, the commercial, the garish, the vile, the reprehensible, and the ugly? Will you follow the much-decorated heroes of fraud and corruption and imitate the flaws of your nation and the flaws of your time? Or will you remember and shine with the glow of expectation and excitement for the possibility of improvement? Will you sit fattened and blinded by a life of conformity and hoarding of wealth, battered and broken by the bone-crushing grip of personal folly, forced to pin all of your most precious and sacred aspirations on the head of a child too young to marry and too light to carry your left-over dreams?

This is a one-time cer-emony. Before you take off your cap and your gown and declare your individual-ity, perhaps through some

It is not money, or fame, or respect, or tradition, or hard work that has brought you here today. It is the blue-edged blade of love, and him cut sharp both ways—the bitter and the sweet.

clichéd and ill-timed act of irreverence, look around and see. Because in this perfect moment, mother and daugh-ter are as one in memory and realization of what was, is, and will be. So as you graduate and momma and grand-momma all beam and shine with the excitement of what is to come, as you celebrate education as a way to achieve greater glory for civilization, all here today under the gloomy skies still possess an eternal optimism unaffected by the passage of time. You hope as your parents hoped and as your children will hope, and all, on a day like this, will be proud.

Now, you have been told that your greatest possession is time; once it's gone you don't get it back. But today it is once again affirmed that your greatest possession is actually optimism. We're optimistic that it will not rain. Optimism is why we wake up all across the globe and initiate sons and daughters and grandkids into the ascendant journey toward knowledge. And this very initiation is also a part of momma and daddy and grandmomma's education, too.

Yes, you are glowing today, grandpa, and someone is going to ask you, "Are you an alumnus?" and you will say, "Connecticut College, Class of '01," and they will think, "Damn! You're old," but they're going to say, "Man, you're looking good, Pops," and you will smile and say, "Thank you." But you realize that these are the last days of babyhood and be ye saint or sinner or both, you see through your generations that what you have done or not done will continue to be not done and done by your sons and grandsons because time does not pass—we do. But we also continue as teachers continue through their students. Shakespeare said it so well: "To be, or not be: that is the question," and the answer is—yes, the great I AM of affirmation.

So realize this, graduates of the great Connecticut College, noble Class of '01: as you pass through time with your righteous anger or unquestioning acceptance of dogma or even indifference to the great spanking board of life that will greet both of your cheeks quite happily and humbly quite soon, it is not money, or fame, or respect, or tradition, or hard work that has brought you here today. It is the blue-edged blade of love, and him cut sharp both ways—the bitter and the sweet. And when he cut you deep in your heart and knock you to your senses, I don't want you to cry or shout or curse. Sing! Sing and make it a song with some soul; make it your song—then you will sing for all of us. The Old Bard said that, too. He said: "To thine own self be true." But, really, the old Mississippi bluesman Hoghead Harris said it best: "It's out there for you, Baby. I got mine."

Strange though it may seem, your education today is the culmination of the education of your parents: the heroic sacrificial act of love that is raising kids ends today! They have put their youngsters through college. So I don't want you all to be too cynical when you look out on your future. We're all here on the last rung of your education, graduate—it is to know yourself and sing for us a song that has never been heard: your song. And when you come to know yourself and to believe in our collective humanity so abundantly evident right here today; when you act on the basis of all the spiritual legacies that have been passed down to us from every corner of the globe, where some kind of song was sung to free the human spirit; when you share your song with us, well, we might just end up feeling as though we are reborn as children,

singing ourselves with such freedom that our lives—
long ago shattered—could sprout new wings and fly.
Once again, in the words of the great bluesman Hoghead
Harris, "Ain't nothing wrong with living, but dying."

So, in closing, I am going to read a poetic passage from
a book entitled *There Is a Tree More Ancient Than Eden*,
written by Leon Forrest. I'm only reading it because
to make a good speech, you have to read some type of
quote. Now, this passage is somewhat difficult to understand, but it speaks of the types of demons that you will
face and it tells us of the optimism that makes life ironic
and transcendent. Place this optimism right next to your
diploma because, believe me, you're going to need it.

> And I shuddered and trembled as we fairly
> floated past this building from which they had
> flown into space: rocketed, sacrificed, yoked
> and bedazzled, raggedy, transfixed, auctioned,
> looted and howling scarecrows into the breath-
> ing jungles of this soft and easy, stormy-out-
> of-Eden country, funky-jawed and joy-ripping,
> grease trapped, babbling wind . . . and in the
> extreme right corner two mammoth blood-
> hounds lapped, tongued and gnawed down the
> bony skeletons and the nostril-gutting spoils
> of this building's bowels bursting like wa-
> ter bags, cast away from its moorings to land-

lostness and humpback prayers spinning amid
hovels and clapboard whispers of dreams and
citadels, psalms, bales of cotton—laughing to
mouth down the bad yoke, which weaves its
way through the house built upon pale riggings
of a vessel afire in a docking bay, which had
become a castle for rats, making potlicker of
the blood, flesh, feces, skeletons, eyes, ears
and throat and tongue of the looted, discarded
shipwrecked spoils in the bowels of the swin-
ish hole . . . Ah but the little children pied-
pipered in their pitch, from where they knew
not/whereof and plunged down singing as if
they were back in the low red-clay country
and stealing up now and winging off, and then
vaulting over the pale ghost of a harpooned
yet thunderously devouring sun in flight—as if
even in their looted youth they were possessed
by wings.

And that's what it's about, Brothers and Sisters. So,
when they ask you, "Where did you come from? When
did you graduate?" and you say, "Connecticut College,
'01," and they think to themselves, "I didn't even know
they had colleges back then," smile to yourself that grim
grin of recognition and know, in the words of the great
bluesman Hoghead Harris, "It's alright, Baby, it's alright."

How to Be Hopeful

Barbara Kingsolver

DUKE UNIVERSITY, 2008

THE VERY LEAST YOU CAN DO IN YOUR LIFE *is to figure out what you hope for. The most you can do is live inside that hope, running down its hallways, touching the walls on both sides.*

Let me begin that way: with an invocation of your own best hopes, thrown like a handful of rice over this celebration. Congratulations, graduates. Congratulations, parents, on the best Mother's Day gift ever. Better than all those burnt-toast breakfasts: these, your children grown tall and competent, educated to within an inch of their lives.

What can I say to people who know almost everything? There was a time when I surely knew, because I'd just graduated from college myself, after writing down the sum of all human knowledge on exams and research papers. But that great pedagogical swilling-out must have depleted my reserves, because decades have passed and now I can't believe how much I don't know. Looking back, I can discern a kind of gaseous exchange in which I exuded cleverness and gradually absorbed better judgment. Wisdom is like frequent-flier miles and scar tissue; if it does accumulate, that happens by accident while you're trying to do something else. And wisdom is what people will start wanting from you, after your last exam. I know it's true for writers—when people love a book, whatever they say about it, what they really mean is: it was *wise*. It helped explain their pickle. My favorites are the canny old codgers: Neruda, García Márquez, Doris Lessing. Honestly, it is harrowing for me to try to teach twenty-year-old students who earnestly want to improve their writing. The best I can think to tell them is: quit smoking, and observe posted speed limits. This will improve your odds of getting old enough to be wise.

If I stopped there, you might have heard my best offer. But I am charged with postponing your diploma for about fifteen more minutes, so I'll proceed, with a caveat. The wisdom of each generation is necessarily new. This tends to dawn on us in revelatory moments, brought to us by our children. For example: My younger daughter is eleven. Every morning, she and I walk down the lane from our farm to the place where she meets the school bus. It's the best part of my day. We have great conversations. But a few weeks ago as we stood waiting in the dawn's early light, Lily was

T he happiest people are the ones with the most community.

quietly looking me over, and finally said: "Mom, just so you know, the only reason I'm letting you wear that outfit is because of your age." The *alleged outfit* will not be described here; whatever you're imagining will perfectly suffice. (Especially if you're picturing *Project Runway* meets *Working with Livestock*.) Now, I believe parents should uphold respect for adult authority, so I did what I had to do. I hid behind the barn when the bus came.

And then I walked back up the lane in my fly regalia, contemplating this new equation: "Because of your age." It's okay now to deck out and turn up as the village idiot. Hooray! I am old enough. How does this happen? Over a certain age, do you become invisible? There is considerable evidence for this in movies and television. But mainly, I think, you're not expected to know the rules. Everyone knows you're operating on software that hasn't been updated for a good while.

The world shifts under our feet. The rules change. Not the Bill of Rights, or the rules of tenting, but the big unspoken truths of a generation. Exhaled by culture, taken in like oxygen, we hold these truths to be self-evident: You get what you pay for. Success is everything. Work is what you do for money, and that's what counts. How could it be otherwise? And the converse of that last rule, of course, is that if you're not paid to do a thing, it can't be important. If a child writes a poem and proudly reads it, adults may wink and ask, "Think there's a lot of money in that?" You may also hear this when you declare a major in English. Being a good neighbor, raising children: the road to success is not paved with the likes of these. Some workplaces actually quantify your likelihood of being distracted by family or volunteerism. It's called your coefficient of Drag. The ideal number is zero. This is the Rule of Perfect Efficiency.

Now, the rule of "Success" has traditionally meant having boatloads of money. But we are not really supposed to put it in a boat. A house would be the customary thing. Ideally it should be large, with a lot of bathrooms and so forth, but no more than four people. If two friends come over during approved visiting hours, the two children have to leave. The bathroom-to-resident ratio should at all times remain greater than one. I'm not making this up, I'm just observing; it's more or less my profession. As Yogi Berra told us, you can observe a lot just by watching. I see our dream houses standing alone, the idealized life taking place in a kind of bubble. So you need another bubble, with rubber tires, to convey yourself to places you must visit, such as an office. If you're successful, it will be a large, empty-ish office you don't have to share. If you need anything, you can get it delivered. Play your cards right and you may never have to come face-to-face with another person. This is the Rule of Escalating Isolation.

And so we find ourselves in the chapter of history I would entitle Isolation and Efficiency, and How They Came Around to Bite Us in the Backside. Because it's looking that way. We're a world at war, ravaged by disagreements, a bizarrely globalized people in which the extravagant excesses of one culture wash up as famine or flood on the shores of another. Even the architecture of our planet is collapsing under the weight of our efficient productivity—our climate, our oceans, migratory paths, things we believed were independent of human affairs. Twenty years ago, climate scientists first told Congress that unlimited carbon emissions were building toward a disastrous instability. Congress said, We need to think about that. About ten years later, nations of the world wrote the Kyoto Protocol, a set of legally binding controls on our carbon emissions. The U.S. said, We still need to think about it. Now we can watch as glaciers disappear, the lights of biodiversity go out, the oceans reverse their ancient orders. A few degrees looked so small on the thermometer. We are so good at measuring things and declaring them under control. How could our weather turn murderous, pummel our coasts, and push new diseases like dengue fever onto our doorsteps? It's an emergency on a scale we've never known. We've responded by following the rules we know: Efficiency, Isolation. We can't slow down our productivity and consumption; that's unthinkable. Can't we just go home and put a really big lock on the door?

Not this time. Our paradigm has met its match. The world will save itself, don't get me wrong. The term "fossil fuels" is not a metaphor or a simile. In the geological sense, it's over. The internal combustion engine is so Twentieth Century. Now we can either shift away from a carbon-based economy, or find another place to live. Imagine it: we raised you on a lie. Everything you plug in, turn on, or drive, the out-of-season foods you eat, the music in your ears. We gave you this world and promised you could keep it running on *a fossil substance*. Dinosaur slime, and it's running out. The geologists only disagree on how much is left, and the climate scientists are now saying they're sorry but that's not even the point. We won't get time to use it all. To stabilize the floods and firestorms, we'll have to reduce our carbon emissions by 80 percent, within a decade.

Heaven help us get our minds around that. We're still stuck on a strategy of bait-and-switch: Okay, we'll keep the cars but run them on ethanol made from corn! But— we use petroleum to grow the corn. Even if you like the idea of robbing the food bank to fill up the tank, there is a math problem: it takes nearly a gallon of fossil fuel to render an equivalent gallon of corn gas. By some accounts, it takes more. Think of the Jules Verne novel in which the hero is racing Around the World in Eighty Days, and finds himself stranded in the mid-Atlantic on a steamship that's run out of coal. It's day seventy-nine. So Phileas Fogg convinces the captain to pull up the decks and throw them into the boiler. "On the next day the masts, rafts and spars were burned. The crew worked lustily, keeping up the fires. There was a perfect rage for demolition." The captain remarked, "Fogg, you've got something of the Yankee about you." Oh, novelists. They always manage to have the last word, even when they are dead.

How can we get from here to there, without burning up our ship? That will be the central question of your adult life: to escape the wild rumpus of carbon-fuel dependency, in the nick of time. You'll make rules that were previously unthinkable, imposing limits on what we can use and possess. You will radically reconsider the power relationship between humans and our habitat. In the words of my esteemed colleague and friend Wendell Berry, the new Emancipation Proclamation will not be for a specific race or species, but for life itself. Imagine it. Nations have already joined together to rein in global consumption. Faith communities have found a new point of agreement with student activists, organizing around the conviction that caring for our planet is a moral obligation. Before the last UN Climate Conference in Bali, thousands of U.S. citizens contacted the State Department to press for binding limits on carbon emissions. We're the 5 percent of humans who have made 50 percent of all the greenhouse gases up there. But our government is reluctant to address it, for one reason: it might hurt our economy.

For a lot of history, many nations said exactly the same thing about abolishing slavery. We can't grant humanity to all people; it would hurt our cotton plantations, our sugar crop, our balance of trade. Until the daughters and sons of a new wisdom declared: We don't care. You have to find another way. Enough of this shame.

Have we lost that kind of courage? Have we let economic growth become our undisputed master again? As we track the unfolding disruption of natural and global stabilities, you will be told to buy into business as usual: You need a job. Trade your future for an entry-level position. Do what we did; preserve a profitable climate for manufacture and consumption, at any cost. Even at the cost of the other climate—the one that was hospitable to life as we knew it. Is anyone thinking this through? In the awful moment when someone demands at gunpoint, "Your money or your life," that's not supposed to be a hard question.

A lot of people, in fact, are rethinking the money answer, looking behind the cash price of everything, to see what it cost us elsewhere: to mine and manufacture, to transport, to burn, to bury. What did it harm on its way here? Could I get it closer to

Imagine getting caught with your Optimism hanging out.

home? Previous generations rarely asked about the hidden costs. We put them on layaway. You don't get to do that. The bill has come due. Some European countries already are calculating the "climate cost" on consumer goods and adding it to the price. The future is here. We're examining the moralities of possession, inventing renewable technologies, recovering sustainable food systems. We're even warming up to the idea that the wealthy nations will have to help the poorer ones, for the sake of a reconstructed world. We've done it before. That was the Marshall Plan. Generosity is not out of the question. It will grind some gears in the machine of Efficiency. But we can retool.

We can also rethink the big, lonely house as a metaphor for success. You are in a perfect position to do that. You've probably spent very little of your recent life in a freestanding unit with a bathroom-to-resident ratio of greater than one. (Maybe more like 1:200.) You've been living so close to your friends, you didn't have to ask about their problems; you had to step over them to get into the room. As you moved from dormitory to apartment to whatever (and by whatever I think I mean Central Campus), you've had such a full life, surrounded by people, in all kinds of social and physical structures, none of which belonged entirely to you. You're told that's all about to change. That growing up means leaving the herd, starting up the long escalator to isolation.

Not necessarily. As you leave here, remember what you loved most in this place. Not Orgo 2, I'm guessing, or the crazed squirrels or even the bulk cereal in the Freshman Marketplace. I mean the way you lived, in close and continuous contact. This is an ancient human social construct that once was common in this land. We called it a community. We lived among our villagers, depending on them for what we needed. If we had a problem, we did not discuss it over the phone with someone in Bhubaneswar. We went to a neighbor. We acquired food from farmers. We listened to music in groups, in churches, or on front porches. We danced. We participated. Even when there was no money in it. Community is our native state. You play hardest for a hometown crowd. You become your best self. You know joy. This is not a guess; there is evidence. The scholars who study social well-being can put it on charts and graphs. In the last thirty years our material wealth has increased in this country, but our self-described happiness has steadily declined. Elsewhere, the people who consider themselves very happy are not in the very poorest nations, as you might guess, nor in the very richest. The winners are Mexico, Ireland, Puerto Rico, the kinds of places we identify with extended family, noisy villages, and a lot of dancing. The happiest people are the ones with the most community. You can take that to the bank. I'm not sure what they'll do with it down there, but you could try.

You could walk out of here with an unconventionally communal sense of how your life may be. This could be your key to a new order: you don't need so much stuff to fill your life, when you have people in it. You don't need jet fuel to get food from a farmers' market. You could invent a new kind of Success that includes children's poetry, butterfly migrations, butterfly kisses, the Grand Canyon, eternity. If somebody says, "Your money or your life," you could say: Life. And mean it. You'll see things collapse in your time, the big houses, the empires of glass. The new green things that sprout up through the wreck—those will be yours.

The arc of history is longer than human vision. It bends. We abolished slavery, we granted universal suffrage. We have done hard things before. And every time it took a terrible fight between people who could not imagine changing the rules and those who said, "We already did. We have made the world new." The hardest part will be to convince yourself of the possibilities, and hang on. If you run out of hope at the end of the day, rise in the morning and put it on again with your shoes. Hope is the only reason you won't give in, burn what's left of the ship, and go down with it—the ship of your natural life and your children's only shot. You have to love that so earnestly—you, who were born into the Age of Irony. Imagine getting caught with your Optimism hanging out. It feels so risky. Like showing up at the bus stop as the village idiot. You may be asked to stand behind the barn. You may feel you're not up to the task.

But think of this: What if someone had dared you, three years ago, to show up to some public event wearing a big, flappy dress with sleeves down to your knees. And on your head, oh, let's say, a beanie with a square board on top. And a tassel! Look at you. You are beautiful. The magic is community. The time has come for the square beanie, and you are rocked in the bosom of the people who get what you're going for. You can be as earnest and ridiculous as you need to be, if you don't attempt it in isolation. The ridiculously earnest are known to travel in groups. And they are known to change the world. Look at you. That could be you.

I'll close with a poem.

HOPE; AN OWNER'S MANUAL

Look, you might as well know, this thing
is going to take endless repair: rubber bands,
crazy glue, tapioca, the square of the hypotenuse.

Nineteenth-century novels. Heartstrings, sunrise:
all of these are useful. Also, feathers.
To keep it humming, sometimes you have to stand
on an incline, where everything looks possible;
on the line you drew yourself. Or in
the grocery line, making faces at a toddler
secretly, over his mother's shoulder.
You might have to pop the clutch and run
past all the evidence. Past everyone who is
laughing or praying for you. Definitely you don't
want to go directly to jail, but still, here you go,
passing time, passing strange. Don't pass this up.
In the worst of times, you will have to pass it off.
Park it and fly by the seat of your pants. With nothing
in the bank, you'll still want to take the express.
Tiptoe past the dogs of the apocalypse that are
    sleeping
in the shade of your future. Pay at the window.
Pass your hope like a bad check.
You might still have just enough time. To make a
    deposit.

To All My Children

Marian Wright Edelman

MUHLENBERG COLLEGE, 2008

THE GREAT GERMAN PROTEST THEOLOGIAN Dietrich Bonhoeffer, who died opposing Hitler's Holocaust, believed
that the test of the morality of a society is how it treats
its children. America flunks Bonhoeffer's test every hour
of every day.

As we let a child drop out of school every ten seconds
of a school day, a child [is] being born in our wealthy nation every thirty-five seconds; a child is being neglected
or abused every thirty-six seconds. Although we lead the
world in health technology, we choose to let a child be
born without health insurance every forty-one seconds.
And every minute, a child has a child, and we let a child

die from gunfire every three hours—eight every day. We have the chronic, quiet equivalent of Virginia Tech every four days. I don't know what it's going to take to have us all stand up and stop the killing of children by guns in the United States of America.

I believe that we have lost our sense of what is important as a people. Too many young people of all races and classes are growing up unable to handle life in hard places, without hope, without steady compasses to navigate a world that is reinventing itself at an unpredictable pace, both technologically and politically. My generation learned that to accomplish anything, we had to get off the dime. Your generation must learn to get off the paradigm over and over, and to be flexible, quick, and smart about it. But, despite all the dazzling change, I believe that there are some enduring values and feel strongly that it is the responsibility of every adult, parent, teacher, preacher, and professional to make sure that young people hear what we have learned from the lessons of life that helped us survive and succeed, to tell you what we think matters, and to [let you] know that you are never alone as you go out to meet the future.

When my sons were graduating from college, I decided to write my older one a letter, a spiritual diary of life lessons. And I'd like to share a few with you. Like them, you can take it or leave it.

Lesson one: there is no free lunch in life. Don't feel entitled to anything you don't sweat and struggle for. Help our nation so that it's not entitled to world leadership based on the past, or on what we say, rather than how well we perform and meet changing world needs.

My generation learned that to accomplish anything, we had to get off the dime. Your generation must learn to get off the paradigm.

For those who are minority in this college class, I hope you will never take anything for granted in America, even with a Muhlenberg degree. And we need to all be concerned as racial intolerance resurges across our land. It may be wrapped up in new euphemisms, and in better etiquette, but as Frederick Douglass warned us earlier, it's the "same old snake."

And for any graduates who feel entitled to leadership by accidental birth or color of skin, let me remind you that the world you already live in is two-thirds nonwhite and poor. And that our nation is becoming a mosaic of greater diversity that you are going to have to understand and respect and work with.

I hope each of you will struggle to continue to achieve and not think for a moment that you've got it made. I know you won't ever be lazy. Do your homework. Pay attention to detail. Take care and pride in your work and take the initiative in creating your own opportunity. And don't wait around for other people to discover you, or do you a favor. Don't assume a door is closed . . . and if it is closed today, don't assume it's closed tomorrow. Keep pushing on it. Don't ever stop learning and improving your mind, because if you do you are going to be left behind.

Lesson two: set thoughtful goals and work quietly and systematically toward them. Don't feel you have to talk if you don't have something important or something that matters to say. Please resist quick-fix, simplistic answers and easy gains, which often disappear just as quickly as they come.

Lesson three: assign yourself. My daddy used to run us crazy when we were children. He asked us every day when we came home from school whether the teacher had given us any homework. When we said "no," he said, "Well, assign yourself some." We shouldn't wait around for our boss or our friends or our spouse to do whatever we are able to do or figure out for ourselves. Don't do just as little as you can to get by. Don't be a political by-stander and grumbler. Please vote, because democracy is not a spectator sport. Don't wait around when you see

a need to ask, "Why doesn't somebody do something?"
Ask, "Why don't I do something?"

Lesson four: please don't work just for money. Money
alone will not save your soul or build a decent family or
help you sleep at night. We are the richest nation on earth
with some of the highest incarceration, drug addiction,
and child poverty rates in the world. Don't ever confuse
wealth or fame with character. And don't condone or tol-
erate moral corruption, whether it's found in high or low
places, whatever its color or class. It's not okay to push or
use drugs even if everybody you know is doing it. It's not
okay to lie or cheat. Be honest. And demand that those
who represent you are honest. Don't confuse morality
with legality. Dr. King once said that everything Hitler
did in Nazi Germany was legal, but it was not right.

**Lesson five: don't be afraid of taking risks or of being
criticized.** If you don't want to be criticized, don't say
anything, don't do anything, and don't be anything.

**Lesson six: take parenting and family life very seri-
ously.** I hope your generation will raise your sons to be
fair to other people's daughters, and to share, and not just
help, with parenting responsibilities. And I hope you will
stress family rituals and be moral examples for your children. If you cut corners, they will too; if you lie, they will

too; if you spend all of your money on yourself and little on your colleges, churches, synagogues, and civic causes, they won't either. And if you tell, or snicker, at racial and gender and gay and lesbian jokes, another generation will pass on the poison that my generation still has not had the courage to snuff out. Stare them down. Make anything that is an attempt to demean another human being unacceptable in your sight.

Last lesson: listen for the genuine within yourself. Albert Einstein said that there are few who see with their own eyes and feel with their own hearts. I hope you will try to be with them, because only those who can find the genuine within themselves can hear it within others.

And never think that life is not worth living. Don't you ever give up. Never cease trying to make a difference. I don't care how hard it gets. You are going to fall down a whole lot of times. It doesn't matter. Keep getting up. There is an old proverb that says when you get to your wit's end, that's where God lives. Hang in there with life. Don't think you have to win immediately, or even at all, to make a difference.

As you go out, I hope you'll remember two things. One of my favorite stories involves my role model Sojourner Truth—who was a fierce feminist or a fierce anti-inequality-for-women person back in slavery, and

she was also against slavery when it seemed hopeless—
who was speaking out against slavery and got heckled by
an old white man in the audience. He said to her: "Old
slave woman, I don't care anymore about your antislavery
talk. It's getting to be like an old flea bite." She replied,
"That's alright; the Lord willing, I'm going to keep you
scratching." So often we think we have to be a big dog,
and we do need big changes. But, you know, enough strategic small fleas can make the biggest dog uncomfortable.

We need to have a new movement that resets the moral
compass for America. But it's going to take a network of
strategic, persistent fleas who don't give up. So I hope
you will be just a flea for justice for children.

Shel Silverstein gets the last word. He said:

Listen to MUSTN'Ts, child.
Listen to the DON'Ts.
Listen to the SHOULDN'Ts,
The IMPOSSIBLEs, the WON'Ts.
Listen to the NEVER HAVEs,
Then listen close to me—
Anything can happen, child.
ANYTHING can be.

If you dream it, if you believe in it, if you struggle for
it, you can never give up. So, Godspeed as you go out and
change the world.

WHO WILL DEFEND THE EARTH?

Noam Chomsky

AMERICAN UNIVERSITY OF BEIRUT, 2013

WITH WRENCHING TRAGEDIES only a few miles away, and still worse catastrophes perhaps not far removed, it may seem wrong, perhaps even cruel, to shift attention to other prospects that, although abstract and uncertain, might offer a path to a better world—and not in the remote future.

I've visited Lebanon several times and witnessed moments of great hope, and of despair, that were tinged with the Lebanese people's remarkable determination to overcome and to move forward. The first time I visited—if that's the right word—was exactly sixty years ago, almost to the day. My wife and I were hiking in Israel's northern

Galilee one evening, when a jeep drove by on a road near us and someone called out that we should turn back: we were in the wrong country. We had inadvertently crossed the border, then unmarked—now, I suppose, bristling with armaments. A minor event, but it forcefully brought home a lesson: the legitimacy of borders—of states, for that matter—is at best conditional and temporary.

Almost all borders have been imposed and maintained by violence, and are quite arbitrary. The Lebanon-Israel border was established a century ago by the Sykes-Picot Agreement, dividing up the former Ottoman Empire in the interests of British and French imperial power, with no concern for the people who happened to live there, or even for the terrain. The border makes no sense, which is why it was so easy to cross unwittingly.

Surveying the terrible conflicts in the world, it's clear that almost all are the residue of imperial crimes and the borders that the great powers drew in their own interests. Pashtuns, for example, have never accepted the legitimacy of the Durand Line, drawn by Britain to separate Pakistan from Afghanistan; nor has any Afghan government ever accepted it. It is in the interests of today's imperial powers that Pashtuns crossing the Durand Line are labeled "terrorists" so that their homes may be subjected to murderous attack by U.S. drones and special operations forces.

Few borders in the world are so heavily guarded by

sophisticated technology, and so subject to impassioned rhetoric, as the one that separates Mexico from the United States, two countries with amicable diplomatic relations. That border was established by U.S. ag-

The legitimacy of borders—of states, for that matter—is at best conditional and temporary.

gression during the nineteenth century. But it was kept fairly open until 1994, when President Bill Clinton initiated Operation Gatekeeper, militarizing it. Before then, people had regularly crossed it to see relatives and friends. It's likely that Operation Gatekeeper was motivated by another event that year: the imposition of the North American Free Trade Agreement, which is a misnomer because of the words "free trade." Doubtless the Clinton administration understood that Mexican farmers, however efficient they might be, couldn't compete with highly subsidized U.S. agribusiness, and that Mexican businesses couldn't compete with U.S. multinationals, which under NAFTA rules must receive special privileges like "national treatment" in Mexico. Such measures would almost inevitably lead to a flood of immigrants across the border.

Some borders are eroding along with the cruel hatreds and conflicts they symbolize and inspire. The most dramatic case is Europe. For centuries, Europe was the most savage region in the world, torn by hideous and destructive wars. Europe developed the technology and the culture of war that enabled it to conquer the world. After a final burst of indescribable savagery, the mutual destruction ceased at the end of World War II. Scholars attribute that outcome to the thesis of democratic peace—that one democracy hesitates to war against another. But Europeans may also have understood that they had developed such capacities for destruction that the next time they played their favorite game, it would be the last. The closer integration that has developed since then is not without serious problems, but it is a vast improvement over what came before.

A similar outcome would hardly be unprecedented for the Middle East, which until recently was essentially borderless. And the borders are eroding, though in awful ways. Syria's seemingly inexorable plunge to suicide is tearing the country apart. Veteran Middle East correspondent Patrick Cockburn, now working for *The Independent*, predicts that the conflagration and its regional impact may lead to the end of the Sykes-Picot regime. The Syrian civil war has reignited the Sunni-Shiite conflict that was one of the most terrible consequences of the U.S.-U.K. invasion of Iraq ten years ago. The Kurdish regions of Iraq and now Syria are moving toward autonomy and linkages. Many analysts now predict that a Kurdish state may be established before a Palestinian state is.

If Palestine ever gains independence in something like the terms of the overwhelming international consensus, its borders with Israel will likely erode through normal commercial and cultural interchange, as has happened in the past during periods of relative calm. That development could be a step toward closer regional integration, and perhaps the slow disappearance of the artificial border dividing the Galilee between Israel and Lebanon, so that hikers and others could pass freely where my wife and I crossed sixty years ago. Such a development seems to me to offer the only realistic hope for some resolution of the plight of Palestinian refugees, now only one of the refugee disasters tormenting the region since the invasion of Iraq and Syria's descent into hell.

The blurring of borders and these challenges to the legitimacy of states bring to the fore serious questions about who owns the earth. Who owns the global atmosphere being polluted by the heat-trapping gases that have just passed an especially perilous threshold, as we learned in May? Or, to adopt the phrase used by indigenous people throughout much of the world, Who will defend the earth? Who will uphold the rights of nature? Who will adopt the role of steward of the commons, our collective possession?

That the earth now desperately needs defense from impending environmental catastrophe is surely obvious to any rational and literate person. The different reactions to the crisis are a most remarkable feature of current history.

At the forefront of the defense of nature are those often called "primitive": members of indigenous and tribal groups, like the First Nations in Canada or the Aborigines in Australia—the remnants of peoples who have survived the imperial onslaught. At the forefront of the assault on nature are those who call themselves the most advanced and civilized: the richest and most powerful nations.

The struggle to defend the commons takes many forms. In microcosm, it is taking place right now in Turkey's Taksim Square, where brave men and women are protecting one of the last remnants of the commons of Istanbul from the wrecking ball of commercialization and gentrification and autocratic rule that is destroying this ancient treasure. The defenders of Taksim Square are at the forefront of a worldwide struggle to preserve the global commons from the ravages of that same wrecking ball—a struggle in which we must all take part, with dedication and resolve, if there is to be any hope for decent human survival in a world that has no borders. It is our common possession, to defend or to destroy.

THE PURSUIT OF MEANINGFULNESS

Toni Morrison

RUTGERS UNIVERSITY, 2011

THIS CEREMONY IS KNOWN AS COMMENCEMENT. Those of you who are graduating, as well as relatives, parents, friends, understand that this moment is also the end—the end of a definitive college experience. But it's not called termination. To commence is to begin—to start something new, to enter new terrain, to launch a career begun here at Rutgers.

I don't intend to dismiss the past in pushing you toward the future, neither your recent years here nor the chaos of the world my generation has left you. I can't dismiss that. We've left you a world in which the earth itself seems to be literally breaking apart—whether dancing to music none of us can hear, distant populations willing to shed red, red blood rather than cower to corrupt dictatorships. Employment is strangely scarce while money rushes—as no river does—up, against gravity.

This is a world where political discourse mimics a Punch and Judy show. And, like that ancient puppet show put on for the masses, it exchanges intelligible language for hits and screams.

"We got it!" / No you don't.

"Get the government off our backs!" / Government must have our backs.

"Women must be free!" / No, women must be directed.

The chaos, as always, is self-contradictory. But we can savor the confusion as the excitement of the new—the post-postmodern, the liberation of the body and the psyche as opportunities for the accumulation of more knowledge, and we can meet disorder with our own humanity.

Rutgers has offered you instruments, strategies of critical thought, contact with fresh ideas to inform your choices and shape your life, but the narrative of a worthy life is yours to write. I have often wished that Jefferson had not used that phrase "the pursuit of happiness" as the third right—although I understand in the first draft it was "life, liberty and the pursuit of property." Of course, I would have been one of those properties one had the right to pursue, so I suppose

Your life is already artful—waiting, just waiting, for you to make it art.

happiness is an ethical improvement over a life devoted to the acquisition of land, acquisition of resources, acquisition of slaves. Still, I would rather he had written life, liberty and the pursuit of meaningfulness or integrity or truth.

I know that happiness has been the real, if covert, goal of your labors here. I know that it informs your choice of companions, the profession you will enter, but I urge you, please don't settle for happiness. It's not good enough. Of course, you deserve it. But if that is all you have in mind—happiness—I want to suggest to you that personal success devoid of meaningfulness, free of a steady commitment to social justice, that's more than a barren life; it is a trivial one. It's looking good instead of doing good.

There is serious work, truly serious work, for you to do. I know you have been blasted with media designed to change you from citizens to consumers, and most recently, simply taxpayers; from a community of engaged civic life, to individuals with hundreds of electronic friends; from a yearning for maturity to a desire for eternal childhood. That's the media's role. But I tell you, no generation, least of all mine, has a complete grip on the imagination and goals of subsequent generations, not if you refuse to let it be so. You don't have to accept media or even scholarly labels for yourself: Generation A, B, C, X, Y, majority, minority, red state, blue state, this social past or that one. Every true heroine breaks free from his or her class—upper, middle, and lower—in order to serve a wider world.

Of course, you're general and you have to function as a group sometimes. But you are also singular. You are a citizen in society and a person like no other on the planet. No one has the exact memory that you have.

So far, no one has your genetic duplicate. These are not paralyzing clashes. They represent the range and the depth of human life. What is now the limit of human endeavor is not the limit of intelligent endeavor. And what is now known is not at all what you are capable of knowing. There is much serious, hard, and ennobling work to do. And, bit by bit, step by step, you can change things—the things that need changing.

Just think of it. It's quite possible that people 100, 200, 300 years from now will be stunned by the things that were taken for granted in 2011 America. They might laugh or shake their heads and wonder with dismay at our notions of progress, justice, and the value of work and of life.

"What?!" they might exclaim, *"You mean to tell me that people back then had to borrow money, work several jobs, save in order to pay for their own education? An education that is the wealth of the nation? I don't believe you. I don't believe you."*

"How could a wealthy nation put the financial burden of improving the [education] level of its own citizens on the marketplace?"

"I know they sold water back then, but did they also require them to pay for clean air?"

"Are you telling me that illness incurred huge personal debt? And that companies were so beholden to profit for their own lives that they could no longer afford health benefits for the lives of their employees?"

"That children, little children, were put in school environments so dangerous no adult would willingly choose to enter them? And, they actually multiplied that danger by allowing them to pack heat in the halls, classrooms, and playgrounds?"

"That females were believed to be too stupid to manage their very own bodies?"

"You mean whole families lived in tunnels and cardboard

boxes on toxic wasteland? That nations watched dead bodies, broken by broken levees, lying on lawns and boulevards providing food for starving dogs?"

Well, perhaps, these people a hundred or more years from now will gasp—recoil as they see that the language at the feet of the Statue of Liberty has been paved over and they discover the dark history of the twenty-first century. Well, maybe not. Maybe not. Perhaps by that time, generations descended from you, taught by you, inspired by you, will have imagined and forged a world worthy of you.

Your education has prepared you for such a leap of imagination and such daring. Rutgers has already offered you opportunities for reflection, innovation—an activity that does gesture toward that world. It's already given you the tools to refine your response to contemporary chaos, to modern unease. You are your own stories, and therefore free to imagine what it takes to remain human with no resources. What it feels like to be a human without domination over others; without fear of others unlike you; without rehearsing and reinventing the hatred learned in the sandbox. Although you don't have complete control of the story of your life, you can still create that story. Although you will never fully know or successfully manipulate all of the characters who surface or disrupt your plot, you can respect the ones you can't avoid by paying them close attention and doing them justice. The plot you choose may change or even elude you, but being your own story means you can control the theme. It also means you can invent the language to say who you are and how you mean in this world.

Well it's true. I am myself a storyteller, and therefore an optimist—a firm believer in the ethical bend of the human heart; a believer in the mind's appetite for truth and its disgust with fraud and selfishness. From my point of view, your life is already a miracle of chance waiting for you to shape its destiny. From my point of view, your life is already artful—waiting, just waiting, for you to make it art.

GO THE DISTANCE

Gloria Steinem

SMITH COLLEGE, 2007

TO THE BELOVED, BRAVE, TIRED, and now headed-for-the-world graduates of the Class of 2007; the first generation of Facebook and YouTube Smithies; the class to shape and survive the most changes in the way Smith lives; the second class of the Iraq War; and the most diverse class in the history of Smith College, from Adas*—who made sure that Class (economic class) Is Never Dismissed—and to all those who help Smith College look more

---

* "Adas" are Ada Comstock scholars, students enrolled in a Smith College program that enables women of nontraditional college age to complete a Bachelor of Arts degree at a realistic pace.

like the world: I thank you for including me in your historic day.

It's historic for me, too, because I was sitting where you sit today exactly fifty-one years ago. I wasn't sure I should bring up this half-century fact. For one thing, I feel connected to you, not distant. For another, I feared you might go into as much age shock as I did when I woke up after my seventieth birthday, and thought, *There's a seventy-year-old woman in my bed! How did this happen?!*

But then I realized that fearing separation by age was probably more my generation's problem than yours. If I conjure up my own graduation day, for instance, even life after thirty seemed a hazy screen to be filled in by the needs of others—and there were not yet even Adas to show us that life and growth continue. In our age ghetto, we pretty much accepted the idea that women were more valued for giving birth to others than for giving birth to ourselves.

Yes, many of us had professions, but they were secondary. As one of my classmates said in the light of later feminism, "I didn't have a job, I had a jobette." We weren't trying to change the world to fit women—and neither was Smith in those days—we were trying to change ourselves to fit the world.

If this seems hard to believe now, think of my two most famous age peers: Marilyn Monroe, who literally feared aging more than death, and Smith's own Sylvia Plath, whose world-class talent couldn't give her the autonomy she needed to survive. Now, thanks to decades of feminist rebellion, your generation is much more likely to value minds and hearts and talents that last just as long as you do. You have not only a somewhat longer life expectancy physically, but faith in a much longer life of your own making. Fortunately for me, this also means you are better able to identify with other women across boundaries of age.

The end doesn't justify the means; the means are the ends.

For instance: My generation of young women said things like, "I'm not going to be anything like my mother." After all, if we didn't blame our mothers for living vicarious lives, we would have to admit that we might have to do the same thing. Even now, my generation—and probably some of yours, too—are living out the unlived lives of our mothers. This is honorable and rewarding and loving, but it isn't the same—for either mother or daughter—as living our own unique lives.

Now, I meet many young women who say something like, "I hope I can have as interesting a life as my mother." Not the *same* life, but *as interesting*. And when I hear this, it brings tears to my eyes—because I know there is not only love between generations, as there always has been, but now there is respect, learning, a sense of balance, even an invitation to adventure and freedom.

So instead of worrying about the decades between us, I thought I would use them as a measure of tomorrow by projecting a similar time into the future. Like the swing of a compass arm, I invite you to measure the progress made in the time between my graduating class and yours, and project into the future the same distance. What might the world be like when you come back to visit the Class of 2057? I'm not suggesting we *know* what will happen, but I am suggesting that imagining is a form of planning.

So let's take a concrete example: In my generation, we were asked by the Smith vocational office how many words we could type a minute, a question that was *never* asked of then all-male students at Harvard or Princeton. Female-only typing was rationalized by supposedly greater female verbal skills, attention to detail, smaller fingers, goodness knows what, but the public imagination just didn't include male typists—certainly not Ivy League–educated ones.

Now, computers have come along, and "typing" is "keyboarding." Suddenly, voila!—men can type! Gives you faith in men's ability to change, doesn't it? So maybe by 2057, occupational segregation—an even greater cause of wage disparity than unequal pay for the same job—may have changed enough so there will be male nurses *and* female surgeons. Then male medics won't come home from the military to be shamed out of good nursing jobs, and nursing will be better paid because it will no longer be a pink-collar ghetto. Also perhaps parking lot attendants will no longer be paid more than child care attendants— as is now the case not because we value our cars more than our children, but because the first are almost totally male and the second are almost totally female.

And most of all, maybe the vast unpaid area of care giving—whether that means raising children or caring for the ill and elderly, it is at least 30 percent of the productive work in this country and more than half in many countries—maybe this huge and vital area of work will at last have an attributed economic value, whether it is done by women or men.

This is already a feminist proposal for tax policy. It would mean the attributed value of caregiving would become tax deductible for those who pay taxes, and tax refundable for those who are too poor to pay taxes, thus substituting for the disaster of welfare. It would be a huge advance. We would at last be valuing all productive work, including that mysteriously defined as not-work—as in homemakers who "don't work," even though they work longer and harder than any other class of worker. (Not to mention with more likelihood of getting replaced by a younger worker.)

Take something deeper: My generation identified

emotionally with every other vulnerable group, but without understanding why. Fifty years later, we understand why: females are an "out" group, too—no wonder we identified. Now, there are local, national, and global liberation movements based on sex, race, ethnicity, sexuality, and class. We know that in these movements we are each other's allies, if only because our adversaries are all the same. Perhaps fifty years from now, the public imagination will finally understand that this is one inseparable movement. The same hierarchy that controls women's bodies as the means of reproduction—which is how we women got into this jam in the first place—and the same one that says that sexuality is only moral when it is directed toward reproduction within patriarchal marriage, also controls reproduction in order to maintain racial difference and to preserve a racist caste system. Then, we will understand better that it's impossible to be a feminist without also being an antiracist—and vice versa. Not only because women are in every group in the world, but because racial caste and sexual caste are intertwined, interdependent, and inseparable.

We will also understand that the same folks who are against contraception and abortion and even the sex education that helps avoid abortion—anything that allows the separation of sexuality from reproduction—are also against sexual expression between two women or between two men. They deny the reality that human sexuality has always been a form of communication and pleasure, not just a way we reproduce. (And I do mean always. The Native women who lived on this very land long before Europeans showed up often had two or three children two or three years apart. They absolutely understood contraception and abortifacients. This is not just some modern gift from the pharmaceutical industry, though it was Margaret Sanger who financed and encouraged such research.)

No wonder antiequality, racist, and antigay forces are all the same, just as they were in, say, Germany under fascism, or in theocracies and totalitarian regimes now. Perhaps fifty years from now, most people will understand that reproductive and sexual freedom—and democratic families, democracy within families—are as necessary to democracy as is the vote and freedom of speech.

Or take another area very close to home. My generation often accepted the idea that the private/public roles of women and men were "natural." Your generation has made giant strides into public life, but often still says: How can I combine career and family? I say to you from the bottom of my heart that when you ask that question you are setting your sights way too low. First of all, there can be no answer until men are asking the same question. Second, every other modern democracy in the world is way, way ahead of this country in providing a national system of child care and job patterns adapted to the needs of parents, both men and women. So don't get guilty. Get mad. Get active. If this is a problem that affects millions of unique women, then the only answer is to organize together.

I know it may be hard for women to believe that men can be loving and nurturing of small children—just as it may be hard for men to believe that women can be as expert and achieving in public life. If you've never seen a deer, it's hard to see a deer. If I hadn't happened to have a father who raised me as a small child as much as my mother did, I might not believe it either. But raising young children—or being raised to raise children—is the way men are most likely to develop their own full circle of human qualities, and to stop reproducing the prison of the "masculine" role, just as our role in the public life frees us of the prison of the "feminine" role. For that matter, our kids do what they see, not what they are told. If children don't see whole people, they're much less likely to *become* whole people—at least, not without a lot of hard work in later life.

Which leads us into the big question of violence. Gender roles provide the slippery slope to the normalization of control and violence in all their forms, from sexualized violence to military violence—which is the distance from A to B. Until the family paradigm of human relationships is about cooperation and not domination or hierarchy, we're unlikely to imagine cooperation as normal or even possible in public life. We must change this paradigm. It is just too dangerous in this era of weapons—especially as it collides with religions that extol Doomsday.

It's already too dangerous in this era when there are more slaves in proportion to the world's population—more people held by force or coercion without benefit from their work—than there were in the 1800s. Sex trafficking, labor trafficking, children and adults forced into armies: they all add up to a global human-trafficking industry that is more profitable than the arms trade, and second only to the drug trade. The big difference now from the 1800s is that the United Nations estimates that 80 percent of those who are enslaved are women and children.

Yes, all this will take much longer than our projected fifty years to transform. The wisdom of original cultures tells us that it takes four generations to heal one violent act. But it's also true that, if we were to raise even one generation of children without violence and without shaming, *we have no idea what might be possible.*

It won't be easy to hang on to this vision of possibilities in ourselves and in others if we are alone in a world that's organized a different way. We are communal creatures. So make sure you're not alone after you leave this community at Smith. Make sure you meet with a few friends once a week or once a month, people you can share experiences and hopes with—and vice versa. Women may need this even more than other marginalized groups because, after all, we will never have our own country (good thing—it makes us antinationalistic); we don't have a neighborhood; most of us don't even have a bar.

If I had one wish for women worldwide, it would be a kind of global version of Alcoholics Anonymous: a network of women's groups—also welcoming to men who have the same radical vision. These leaderless and free groups would exist in cities and villages, in school basements and around rural wells. They could spread like lace over the globe and their purpose would be to support self-authority. After all, democracy can't exist without the female half of the world's population.

While we're at it over the next fifty years, remember that the end doesn't justify the means; the means *are* the ends. If we want joy and music and friendship and laughter at the end of our revolution, we must have joy and music and friendship and laughter along the way. Emma Goldman had the right idea about dancing at the revolution.

So, my beloved comrades, yes this is the longest of all revolutions and that will mean a lot of struggle, a lot of organizing together and a lot of unity, but that also means a lot of dancing.

For now, just measure the distance from my graduation to yours—from my class with only one student of color to your diverse class, from my era of no women's history to yours that has been strengthened by women's history.

You will see that you can match or surpass that distance that we have covered.

Now, it's true that I have every intention of living to be a hundred. But even I, hope-oholic that I am, know that when you return to celebrate your victories and inspire the Class of 2057, I won't be with you.

But then again: I will.

THE WORLD IS WAITING FOR YOU

Tony Kushner

VASSAR COLLEGE, 2002

THE LAST TIME I attended a college commencement—
it was a couple of years ago and I won't say where—the
commencement speaker was an associate justice of the
U.S. Supreme Court; I won't say which one but it wasn't
one of the really scary justices, not one of the ones who
jimmied open a window in the White House and gave
you-know-who a leg up as he clambered his ungainly way
into the Oval Office. This justice was one of the other
ones. Instead of offering to the matriculants the usual
bromides, advice, or inspiration, Associate Justice X took
the opportunity to read aloud bad reviews of some of the
decisions he'd delivered, and to respond to the reviews at

considerable length, even though I don't think any of the critics who'd written the reviews were present at this graduation ceremony. I was sort of touched by his speech because it had never occurred to me that justices' decisions are reviewed just as plays are reviewed, and that justices probably hate critics as much as playwrights do, at least as much as this playwright does, at least the moronic wicked corrupt critics who criticize me. Associate Supreme Court Justice X had brought with him a huge black ring binder full of bad reviews, each review carefully preserved under plastic, and it had about it the aspect of being frequently and lingeringly perused, this binder did. And the commencement speech had about it the quality of a grudge match, of a settling of scores. It was not inspirational or uplifting. But I was sympathetic. I found it honest and brave and instructive-by-example: even if you rise as high in life as an associate justice of the Supreme Court you will be pursued by critics as the damned are pursued by fiends in hell, and you will find yourself grumbling embarrassingly about their reviews, grumbling in inappropriate places, dampening festive occasions. I assume the point the justice was making, by example, was this: "See, graduating students! It never ends! You will be graded forever! And YOU WILL NEVER BE HAPPY!" The applause after Justice X finished his grim tuition was suitably ashy; but then, under the smiling blue skies of May, under the woozy influence of the heatstroke which perennially adds its charm to graduation ceremonies, everyone promptly forgot everything the commencement speaker had spoken and that giddy graduation mood compounded of jubilation, accomplishment, bankruptcy, terror, and exhaustion carried the day to its traditional sunshiny apotheosis.

What am I doing here? One of the answers ought to be: I am here to organize. I am here to be political.

I enjoy commencement because it's a summery affair, a warm-weather ceremony of liberation, lovely young people frantic to feel for the first time since toddlerhood what it's like to be a person rather than a student—and I don't want to harsh anyone's buzz or whatever it is you say nowadays, but when you're eighty you will still be waiting to find out what it's like to be a person rather than a student; even if you haven't been a student for fifty-nine years you will still feel more like a student than a person, because in this country, in this world, the only thing we do worse than education is life. Vassar being the great exception to this, I must stipulate to that, I can tell just by looking at you not only how thoroughly and capaciously and meticulously you have been prepared for matriculation, but also how fantastically lively you all are; you are radiant, each and every one of you, your parents are *shepping* major *naches* at how radiant and formidable you have become, they're maybe not entirely sure why this effect was so expensive to produce, but looking at you robed and mortarboarded and aflame with vision, ambition, and hope, they are certain it was worth every penny and each drop of spilled blood and they look forward to long years exacting their subtle and exquisitely costly vengeance. They have earned this vengeance, your parents, so you should not complain too much. It will build your character, which, even after four years at Vassar, may yet face further construction and benefit from it.

I *hope* you are aflame with vision, ambition, and hope. I came here expecting to get a contact high from you; what a bummer it would be to discover that you are not aflame, that you have managed on this day of days merely to smolder! A bummer but not a surprise, I mean who could blame you, really; hasn't this past year, *your senior year*, been the worst year ever in the history of humankind? Maybe it's the beginning of the end of the world, but please, you should not feel personally responsible. Blame someone else. Blame your parents. Why not? They are blaming your grandparents. Or blame the Bush administration, that's what I do; if that gets old, blame Ralph Nader. And Happy Graduation!

What to say to the graduating class of 2002, to you vibrant young people leaving college and entering the great world beyond just in time to be trampled flat by the Four

Horsemen of the Apocalypse? "Duck!" might be a good place to start. "Stockpile canned goods and huge vats of water." Beyond that, what to say? I could read some bad reviews I've gotten. I don't have a ring binder, but I have several of the most malicious committed to memory. It would be a chance for payback for the critics I particularly dislike. But this can hardly be the reason you've invited me. If you'd wanted bitterness, you could have asked a Supreme Court justice. There are nine of them and each is more bitter than the next, except for the one who likes to lead group sing-a-longs featuring songs of the Old South sung in funny accents. He isn't bitter, just terribly alarming. You could have invited him, but you didn't. Neither kvetching nor Stephen Foster were what you wanted to hear in this speech, among the last words you will hear before you are officially diploma-ed and commenced.

You wanted to hear from a playwright, at least some of you did, at least someone at Vassar did, unless a mistake has been made and you actually meant to invite Tony Kushner the British Holocaust historian. He might have been a better choice, Holocaust with either a big or little "H" being something we all have to think about constantly during these very dark days. If you meant to invite me, and let's proceed from that assumption, then you wanted a playwright and I have to say what a strange choice, what with Gabriel blowing his trumpet and the Book of Revelation unfolding seal by seal and all. It's as if you'd been warned of years of calamity and famine ahead and in response you anxiously stuffed an after-dinner mint in your pocket. You *should* have gotten the British Tony Kushner, or maybe Condoleezza Rice, who is I believe actually mentioned in the Book of Revelation—I know Stanford University is mentioned, I know her boss is mentioned, I know John Ashcroft features prominently, and not pleasantly, with bat wings and horns. *Really*, you can look it up. This is a time of crisis and in a time of crisis we all have to focus on getting real, and you, what do you do? You get a playwright to deliver the 2002 commencement speech.

Thank you for inviting me, but I worry about you. Haven't you been reading the papers? Weren't your parents worried when you told them who'd be speaking? Didn't they suggest you go in another direction, maybe get someone who could explain to you how the new arms reduction agreement Bush and Putin just signed—which seems to me to leave the number of intact nuclear warheads unchanged but allows Bush to go ahead and begin building Star Wars, which seems to me proliferation rather than disarmament—you could maybe get someone to explain how this is *good* news and an improvement over an actual arms reduction treaty. I would have bought a ticket to Poughkeepsie just to hear someone explain that. Am I some sort of gesture, some louche trilled cadenza sung while the ship goes under? Am I a symptom of your despair, and if I am, why couldn't you have gone for something a bit more techno-savvy? Someone from the movies, Spiderman for instance. Why someone from the *theater*, for God's sake; do you want everyone to think you're gay?

Is *that* it? Is it because I'm gay? Did you hope to shock your grandparents? But you know, since the Bush administration began issuing those warnings every ten minutes that more terror is on its way and we apparently can't do Thing One about it, I have been feeling incredibly uninterested in sex. And anyway I am a very old-fashioned kind of homosexual, or rather sexual minoritarian. I am the kind of homosexual sexual minoritarian who believes that sexual minoritarian liberation is inextricable from the grand project of advancing federally protected civil rights, and cannot be separated from the liberation struggles of other oppressed populations, cannot be achieved isolated from the global struggle for the abolition of the legacy of colonialism, cannot be achieved isolated from the global resistance movement against militarism and imperialism and racism and fundamentalisms of all sorts, the global movement for the furtherance of social and economic justice, the global multiculturalist antitribalist identity-based movement for pluralist democracy. I am the kind of homosexual who believes that all liberation has an inexpungible aspect that is collective, communitarian, and also millenarian, utopian, which is to say rooted in principle, theory, dream, imagination, in the absolute non-existence of the Absolute and in the eternal existence of

the Alternative, of the Other, in the insistently unceas-
ingly mutable character of our character. I am an old-
fashioned sort of homosexual/sexual minoritarian, and
I think if you wanted a gay commencement speaker in
this dark day and age you might have chosen one of those
newfangled neocon gay people with their own website
and no day job. This is a world in which the Netherlands
becomes the latest European country to lurch to the anti-
immigrant anti-Muslim Right through the offices of a gay
politician assassinated by an infuriated vegan anti-mink-
farming gun-toting lunatic. I am simply too old-fashioned
and maybe just too *old* to explain to you how we got from
Stonewall to Pim Fortuyn. I'm still trying to understand
how it is that I pay taxes but I can't marry my boyfriend,
but I bet you can get the Netherlands and more explained
for you on http-backslash-backslash neocongaypundit.
com, and maybe you could have gotten that guy, you
know, whatsisname, to come to explicate further the future we face of new crusades and the clash of cultures,
and how laws against discrimination and hate crimes are
actually bad for gay people.

Perhaps you asked me to make this speech because I
am a working artist and many of you are—graduates-to-
be and their parents alike—wondering about the market
value of this diploma you're about to get as you contemplate a career in the arts. Vassar has a, well, you know,
arty reputation, so I imagine some of you are thinking

of careers in the arts and you picked me to come talk to you today to give you advice about making a living as an artist. What I usually say, when asked, is "Go for it" and "Be prepared for the day when the devil knocks on your door." Making a living is much easier than getting a bachelor's degree, and much more of a sure thing than surviving 'til 2003; but the bit about the devil is the tricky part, and I wonder if maybe you should have asked a rabbi or a minister or an imam, who would, had you done so, probably be standing here telling you that if avoiding doing deals with the devil is important to you, maybe you could find a field somewhat less proximate to the infernal realms than the arts.

WHAT AM I DOING HERE is I guess my question, and it seems to me that it's a good question to ask in a commencement speech. WHAT AM I DOING HERE, or perhaps another way of putting it, WHY ME? A very useful question, two simple words which, depending on their inflection, can express everything from dark-night-of-the-soul-delving to adenoidal self-pitying whininess, either one of which is suitable to the occasion of graduating from college. WHY ME? WHAT AM I DOING HERE? Perhaps you invited me to do the speech because you know no one in the theater would have the poor taste to try to answer a question like that.

You could ask your parents WHY ME if in asking you mean how did I come to be like this; they, after all, made you, at least some of you. No one will ask them to take responsibility for the whole of you, but if in asking WHY ME you are inquiring after the specifics of your specificity, WHY AM I ME AND NOT SOMEONE ELSE, you could begin by looking into your origins. Some of the answers can be found in your home, and by setting the answers you glean through observation, coercion, and psychoanalytic psychotherapy in a dialectical spin with the facts of your place in history, in time, your place in the world at large, in the culture which is your larger context, in the ideology you have inherited and I hope transformed by living and which with your psyche is the prism through which your self or your soul is refracted, the light and air baffle which your flame or the smoke from your smoldering traverses to reach the exterior world, by setting the inner and the outer up as combatants on the epic dramatic stage in your head, you will arrive, maybe by the time you're eighty, maybe earlier if you work hard at it, at some understanding of yourself—if you don't fear the dark night of the soul, you will, and you won't fear it so much as long as you remember that no one is happy, only Bush is happy. The best you can hope for is to be happyish; remember, too, that the real value of a dark night of the soul is that it's maybe the surest way of ascertaining that you have one, a soul that is. A few rare souls are genuinely native to daylight, but in my experience most of us, if we have souls, have the nocturnal kind; they aren't dark, but darkness may be their element, darkness is a comfort to anything so divided against itself. There, see! Who needs a rabbi?

Only date people who have read a different set of books than you have read; it will save you lots of time in the library.

Having some answer to the WHY ME question, having done the work to change the way you inflect that question from the adenoidal to the introspective, is useful as you try to answer the other question, WHAT AM I DOING HERE, a question which vast forces of reaction— otherwise known as the devil, the Republican Party, the petrochemical industry, Dick and Lynn Cheney, call them what you will—vast and nearly ineluctably persuasive and pervasive forces of reaction will seek to answer for you: you are here to consume and to surrender. You are here to comply, to be in agreement. You are not, these agents of sin and of Satan will tell you, here to *do* anything, or rather you are not here to ask *what to do*, or *why*. The only action, the only agency permissible, is the secret compact of compliance you are expected to make with an order so vast it is nearly invisible, the secret surrender you are expected to have made of your own specificity in the name of an antihuman unjust antiegalitarian antidemocratic ideology that masks its brutality in the guise of an Individualism that enforces conformity and a Freedom that exists within a desperately circumscribed arena of economic terror, scarcity, and selfishness.

What you are doing here is knowing never to ask the question WHAT AM I DOING HERE in such a way that your perilous security is imperiled, in such a way that your civilization's failure to provide for you anything like a civilized security, safety, luxury, home, is exposed through your asking and answering. This has always been true, as I'm sure you have learned in your classes, and in your lives. There have always been these forces, these imps and demons, this terror. But you graduate into a world in which the terror has become exponentially greater; though its aim is essentially unchanged, its aim remains the preservation of the global economy of violence and oligarchy, the preservation of grotesquely unequal distribution of the world's wealth and the human services and societal and cultural infrastructures that go with wealth. Its aim remains the perpetuation of the tragedies of unequal development, its aim remains injustice, and though it doesn't even know it itself, it is one of the four horsemen of the apocalypse.

The answers you provide for yourself to the question WHY ME will be of great consequence to the way you answer WHAT AM I DOING HERE, but if I may succumb to the immemorial nasty habit of commencement speakers since back in the days when the robes you are wearing were street clothes, and offer you advice. One of the answers to the WHAT question ought to be: I am here to organize. I am here to be political. I am here to be a citizen in a pluralist democracy. I am here to be effective, to have agency, to make a claim on power, to spread it around, to rearrange it, to democratize it, to legislate it into justice.

Why you? Because the world will end if you don't act. You are the citizen of a flawed but actual democracy. Citizens are not actually capable of not acting; it is not given to a citizen that she doesn't act. This is the price you pay for being a citizen of a democracy. Your life is married to the political beyond the possibility of divorcement. You are always an agent. When you don't act, you act. When you don't vote, you vote. When you accept the loony logic of some of the left that there is no political value in supporting the lesser of two evils, you open the door to the greater evil. That's what happens when you despair; you open the door to evil, and evil is always happy to enter, sit down, abolish the Clean Air Act and the Kyoto accords, and refuse to participate in the World Court or the ban on land mines. Evil is happy refusing funds to American clinics overseas that counsel abortion, and evil is happy drilling for oil in Alaska. Evil is happy pinching pennies while 40 million people worldwide suffer and perish from AIDS; and evil will sit there, carefully chewing pretzels and fondly flipping through the scrapbook reminiscing about the 131 people he executed when he was governor, while his wife reads Dostoyevsky in the corner. Evil has a brother in Florida and a whole bunch of relatives. Evil settles in and it's the devil of a time getting him to vacate. Look at the White House. Look at France, look at Italy, Austria, the Netherlands. Look at Israel. See what despair and inaction on the part of citizens produces. Act! Organize. It's boring, but do it. The world ends if you don't.

And as long as I have slipped and am offering advice, here's some more: Don't smoke, are you crazy? Don't take drugs. Aren't there enough chemicals in your shampoo and your apples and your air and your antihistamine? Don't drink, it makes you sloppy. Don't drive an SUV, are you crazy? Don't make deals with the devil. Don't even do lunch with the devil. Don't even take his phone calls; he wants you to write a screenplay for him and he wants to give you NOTES.

Will the world end if you act? Will the world end anyway even if you find an organization, stuff envelopes, give money, organize? Maybe. Quite possibly. These are monstrous times and there's no telling. Look across the globe. When have you ever seen such a dismaying crew in occupation of every seat of power? A certifiable nutcase here, a tin-pot dictator there, a feckless blood-spattered plutocrat in this office, an unindicted war criminal in that office, miscreants, meshuginahs, maniacs, and every one of them has the means of doing the most appalling damage. You aren't fundamentalists. You have had a superb education and you have learned how to read; you have learned that all reading is interpretation. You are smart readers but we've failed miserably to educate the world and so there are many poor readers out there, many fundamentalists, and every one of them has the means of doing the most appalling damage. Everyone who wants to can do quite a lot toward bringing the world to an end. But hope isn't a choice, it's a moral obligation, it's a human obligation, it's an obligation to the cells in your body. Hope is a function of those cells; it's a bodily function the same as breathing and eating and sleeping. Hope is not naïve; hope grapples endlessly with despair. Real vivid powerful thunderclap hope, like the soul, is at home in darkness, is divided. But lose your hope and you lose your soul, and you don't want to do that, trust me. Even if you haven't got a soul, and who knows, you shouldn't be careless about it.

Will the world end if you act? Who can say? Will you lose your soul, your democratic citizen soul, if you don't act, if you don't organize? I guarantee it. And you will feel really embarrassed at your ten-year class reunion. People will point, I promise you; people always know when a person has lost his soul. And no one likes a zombie, even if, from time to time, people will date them.

The great Polish poet Czeslaw Milosz has a poem entitled "On Angels"—you can imagine why I was drawn to it—and it concludes by articulating the best possible answer to WHAT AM I DOING HERE and WHY ME. The poet is haunted by a voice:

I have heard that voice many a time when asleep
and, what is strange, I understood more or less
an order or an appeal in an unearthly tongue:
day draws near
another one
do what you can.

The first time I had to give a commencement speech
I was so nervous. I'd been dating this guy, not a zombie,
a nice guy, a grad student in Victorian literature—here's
another piece of advice: only date people who have read
a different set of books than you have read; it will save
you lots of time in the library—and I told him I didn't
know what to say in this commencement speech, and he
said, "You ought to look at Emerson's commencement
address to the Harvard Divinity School," and I said, "Oh
of course, I *love* that." And here's my last piece of advice: *never* admit to not having read something. So I went
home and read it, and it's so beautiful and so true that I
was blocked from writing for several weeks. It's so beautiful and true that after Emerson delivered it, Harvard
refused to let him back on campus for thirty years.

The address begins so beautifully I must to read it to
you.

In this refulgent summer, it has been a luxury
to draw the breath of life. The grass grows, the
buds burst, the meadow is spotted with fire

and gold in the tint of flowers. The air is full
of birds, and sweet with the breath of the pine,
the balm-of-Gilead, and the new hay. Night
brings no gloom to the heart with its welcome
shade. Through the transparent darkness the
stars pour their almost spiritual rays. Man under them seems a young child, and his huge
globe a toy. The cool night bathes the world
as with a river, and prepares his eyes again for
the crimson dawn. The mystery of nature was
never more happily displayed.

And even in rough tough butch Poughkeepsie, even
under stormy skies, one hundred and twenty-seven years
of additional environmental despoliation later, we still
know what Emerson is talking about.

And then he goes on to say many many extraordinary
things, and you should all read Emerson, all the time,
talk about a soul divided, talk about a bright soul living
in darkness, but I thought this would make a perfect way
to conclude. For what better advice could one offer to
graduates, to citizen souls, than this:

"But speak the truth," says Ralph Waldo Emerson, "and all nature and all spirits help you
with unexpected furtherance. Speak the truth,
and all things alive or brute are vouchers, and

the very roots of the grass underground there, do seem to stir and move to bear you witness. Good is positive. Evil is merely privative. It is like cold, which is the privation of heat. All evil is so much death and nonentity. Benevolence is absolute and real. The intuition of the moral sentiment is an insight of the perfection of the laws of the soul. The dawn of the sentiment of virtue on the heart gives and is the assurance that Law is sovereign over all natures; [But speak the truth] and the worlds, time, space, eternity, do seem to break out into joy."

It's time to stop talking. Oh, it always goes like this— I start out not knowing what to say and before I know it I can't shut up. So commence already! A million billion mazels to you and your parents and your teachers and Vassar for having done so self-evidently magnificent a job. I am certain you are aflame. Hurry hurry hurry, now now now, damn the critics and the bad reviews: the world is waiting for you! Organize. Speak the truth.

ALLOW HOPE BUT ALSO FEAR

Chimamanda Ngozi Adichie

KALAMAZOO COLLEGE, 2009

I MUST START BY SAYING that I feel a little bit like a pretender to the throne, standing here before you in this interesting robe. When I received the very gracious invitation, I felt both honored and also quite daunted. I wasn't sure I would be any good at dispensing the kind of pithy and ultimately feel-good wisdoms that are the trademarks of commencement speeches. And this really isn't the best of times for the usual clichéd wisdoms of commencement speeches.

I read somewhere that one of my favorite writers, Kurt Vonnegut, was once asked to give a commencement address. So he came up and said these words to the graduating class: "Everything is going to become un-imaginably worse, and never get better again." And then walked off the stage. Now I considered doing that, but I thought it probably wouldn't be such a good idea.

I remember when I first came here to Kalamazoo, in the autumn of 2005 when you read my novel *Purple Hibiscus* as your common book. You were freshmen and you *were* fresh in many ways, green in the best possible sense, trusting and naïve, forward-looking and secure that the universe would remain as you imagined it. I also thought you were open-minded, eager to learn, full of possibility.

And now here you are, amazing class of 2009, older by four years and hopefully wiser. You have probably done some drinking, some studying; you might have fallen in love or been heartbroken; you've made friendships that will last and some that will not; you've read books you might never have read; you've done internships and study abroad; and most of all, you've become much more privi-leged than you were when I met you four years ago. It doesn't matter what your personal circumstance is. It doesn't matter that you may not find a job tomorrow but instead will have to go to grad school or move into your parents' basement. You are still very privileged. Because by having graduated from Kalamazoo College—a safe place where you are made aware of your choices, where you have small class sizes and a wonderful library and every imaginable resource, a place where ideas rule, but a place aware enough of the world's practicalities to immerse you in its experiential model of education, a place so aware of our global connection that you have a high number of graduates going on to the Peace Corps, a place where you are taught to think independently, a place where you learn self-

You'll trip many times. Don't be surprised when you fall. Maybe even lounge in the dirt a little. And then, get up!

confidence without being aware that you are learning self-confidence—you are privileged. You are immensely privileged.

Four years ago when I first met you, I'm sure none of you ever imagined that you would be graduating in a rather inauspicious year. This is the year that the economic order of the world is coming apart at the seams. Unemployment is the highest it has been in four decades. This is the year that the big banks of America took taxpayer money. This is the year that the major companies that we thought invincible are filing for bankruptcy. This is the year that the news has become about economic apocalypse. This is the year that the world is rethinking the very institutions central to its identity. And this is the year that you are graduating.

An American friend recently told me that because of

the economic downturn, she had stopped eating out at restaurants. And I told her about my aunt in my hometown in eastern Nigeria who has had to close her tiny shop because of the economic downturn and who would probably starve if she didn't have family members to support her. Things are bad, but "bad" is always relative. We live in a world of inequality, gross inequality. While one person in one part of the world stops eating at restaurants because of the economic downturn, another confronts the possibility of not eating at all. And to remind you of this is to remind you of your privilege—not only because it comes with responsibility, but because it is important for you to keep things in perspective.

I've noticed that people who give commencement addresses are usually people who are supposed to have it all figured out. I'm afraid I haven't. And so instead of giving you the secret formula to a perfect life—which I really wish I had because I certainly need it myself—I'd like to end with some random suggestions I have accumulated at the grand age of almost thirty-two.

Suggestion 1: Please think about what you want to value. I remember when I first came to the U.S., twelve years ago now, and I was struck by how often people talked about suing somebody. My friend once slipped and fell on the snow and the first thing she said when she got up, half joking, was who can I sue and get tons of money?

Now, I come from a country that has a justice system that does not always protect the individual, so I appreciated this kind of protection, on the one hand, but on the other hand, it made me think about what was given value in this society. People would say, Oh, there was medical malpractice and a loved one died but the family sued and got a lot of money. There was, I thought, too much value given to the idea of money as substitute for loss, for pain, for emotion. Now, money is of course very important and can change the world for the better, but now that you have that diploma, think about creating a society, an organization, a company that values the things that you want to value rather than the things that you are supposed to value.

Suggestion 2: Please read books. And I don't say this because I am a writer who needs to earn a living (well, that's not the ONLY reason!), but because books are still the best ways to truly come close to understanding complexity in our very complex world. When we read, as my friend the brilliant Irish writer Colum McCann put it, we become alive in bodies not our own. It seems to me that we live in a world where it has become increasingly important to try and live in bodies not our own, to embrace empathy, to constantly be reminded that we share, with everybody in every part of the world, a common and equal humanity.

Suggestion 3: Please remember that there is never a single story about anything. I once spoke at a university in Oklahoma (I didn't have as much fun there as I did at "K," by the way) and a well-meaning student had read *Purple Hibiscus* and said that it was such a shame that Nigerian men were like the abusive father character. I replied that I had just read a novel called *American Psycho* by Bret Easton Ellis and that it was a shame that all young Americans were serial murderers. Obviously I said this in a fit of irritation. But it would never have occurred to me to think that just because I had read a novel about a young American character, he was somehow representative of all Americans. This is not because I am a better person than that student—a very unlikely prospect—but because I had read Gaitskill and Faulkner and Roth and Tyler. Because I had many stories of America. Please try as much as you can to have many stories of the world.

Suggestion 4: Please think about how little you know. Leave room in your mind to revise opinions, to avoid smugness. It is very easy to become smug when you've gone to a good college like "K" and have that gleaming diploma. I know from experience. Like you, I have been fortunate to have a good education and there are times when I feel the smugness creeping up as a result of it and I have to shove it back! I hope that your diploma will remind you of what you still don't know. After my second novel, *Half of a Yellow Sun* (*HOAYS*), which is about the Nigeria-Biafra conflict, was published, I decided to go back to graduate school to study African history. I was often asked why I had, because I had written a novel that was taught as African history. And I remember thinking that I went back to school because I woke up each morning realizing how little I knew and how much I wanted to know.

Suggestion 5: Please make room for hope and for fear. Here's a story about fiction. I've often imagined that fiction and faith are very alike—faith in God, faith in humanism, faith in the power of good. To write fiction is to jump into this journey not knowing where it will end but wanting to go on the journey anyway. To write fiction is to start a long walk knowing you will trip and fall down many times but are still keen to take the walk. I cannot tell you how many times, in the course of writing *HOAYS*, which was a deeply emotional book for me, I felt filled with terror, with uncertainty, with fear. I would climb into bed and eat lots of ice cream. But I knew, because I had made this choice to write fiction, that after all the ice cream bingeing, after all the dark and deep depression, that I would get up and keep writing. It seems to me that this is not a bad way to look at the rest of your life.

You'll trip many times. Don't be surprised when you fall. Maybe even lounge in the dirt a little. And then, get up! Congratulations again. I wish you a life filled with meaning and laughter.

ON EMPATHY AND REASON

Paul Farmer

UNIVERSITY OF DELAWARE, 2013

I.

IT'S A PLEASURE TO be at "YoUDee" on the day you and your families mark the end of your studies here and take your next steps into lives as business folk, nurses, economists, physicists, applied mathematicians, physical therapists, teachers, psychologists, fellow anthropologists, et cetera. It's a pleasure to be here as you begin your first days of freedom before resuming, as some of you will, studies in different and more specialized fields. And then of course some of you are not entirely sure what you'll be doing or where you'll be going. To be honest, it's not that you aren't "entirely sure" but rather that you have no clue. A lot of you are about to join, in the eyes of your parents and however briefly, the ranks of the unemployed. But it's okay (and I say this to the parents): you've got that UD diploma.

If you're worried or disgruntled, you can hardly blame *me* for the state of our economy. This plausible deniability is one of the advantages of being a commencement speaker who is not a high-ranking official or former titan of Wall Street. Yes, I know you wanted President Obama as your speaker, but he's busy. Or Joe Biden, but he's been here, done this. Or Oprah, but she's doing the Harvard commencement. Or a rock star, but they don't get up this early. So you get me, an infectious disease doctor and anthropologist who works mostly in far-off places and who is interested, primarily, in the health and well-being of the poorest and most vulnerable, some of them to be found right here in this country.

Many of you have guessed, already, that I will be talking about this very subject, hardly the usual fare in a graduation address. When you do enough of these speeches, especially about difficult topics, you look for inspiration where you can get it. Inspiration isn't always in ready supply, and so every year at this time I get anxious about writing something new and memorable for a broad audience, a large fraction of which is hoping for the burdensome trifecta of brevity and entertainment and originality. (Granted, some care only about the brevity part, as I

learned during a dinner supposedly in my honor and
for Professor Hummel and
President Zhu. A couple of
high-ranking officials, who
will go unnamed since they
are in close proximity and
could be packing heat under
their robes, made a few too
many brevity jokes.)

I know you wanted President Obama as your speaker, but he's busy. Or a rock star, but they don't get up this early.

But there's no such thing as a stump speech for gradu-
ations, a challenge further complicated when the basic
topic, if not the stories, *is* the same each year. Imagine
for a minute what *health equity* might look like for an anthropologist who is also a doctor. Working in places like
Haiti and Rwanda and Lesotho and Malawi, and also at a
Harvard teaching hospital, reminds me of the social and
cultural particularities of each time and place. But the
sicknesses we see—AIDS, tuberculosis, malaria, road
trauma, cancer—vary less than you might think. The
chest X-rays look the same, as do lab results; the physical examination of these patients is the same from one
place to another. The stigmata of malnutrition are grimly
similar wherever its cause is not having enough to eat.
Even the aspirations of our patients—to feel better, to be
cured, to be heard, to help friends and family members,
to get back to work, or to return to school—all are often

strikingly familiar from place to place. Too many of these aspirations are dashed not only by serious illness but also by poverty. Both need to be attacked.

And so I end up speaking, in every commencement address, about the need for you graduates, and for all of us, to be involved in efforts to make this world a better place. I recently published a book of these speeches and was interviewed two weeks ago by Charlie Rose, a thoughtful fellow with a television show. He liked the book, he said, but also made a rather annoying suggestion for my next commencement speech, which of course happens to be this one today. "Why don't you just make it short and say the following: There's too much unnecessary suffering in the world. Go out and fix it."

He chuckled at his own joke. Quite a bit.

I squirmed, and offered Mr. Rose and his viewers a nervous reply: "Well, the students would cheer its brevity." I opened my mouth for an erudite riposte, something about how Lincoln's most famous speech came in at slightly less than 300 words, but Charlie had moved on.

Dear graduates, I'm afraid I can't say much of anything in 300 words, which is why I write books and articles rather than tweet my thoughts. So don't expect the Gettysburg Address. You have, as your speaker, neither a president nor a rock star. But I'd like to think you UD folks wouldn't have me come all this way for concision alone. So here's some good news: I will be making, today, an Important Announcement. "Dare to be first," as the UD motto goes, and I've chosen this very day, your graduation, to announce my discovery and naming of a new disease, which I've elected to call EDD. That

Can unstable emotions like empathy and compassion be transformed into something more enduring? Yes.

stands for *Empathy Deficit Disorder*. I'm also announcing today a cure for EDD, which I will lay out for you and for reporters wishing to cover this breaking news in nonclinical terms by telling a story about the struggle between empathy and reason. This narrative does in fact involve a rock star, and even a couple of presidents and other leaders, among whom EDD has, at times, reached epidemic proportions. Curing EDD among *leaders*, which many of you will become, will help untold millions whose unnecessary suffering may be averted or cured as long as our efforts are supported by a broad-based coalition of people able to link empathy to reason and action. That's my diagnosis and here's my prescription: we need to be part of that coalition. Since I'm the brilliant fellow who first discovered and announced, right here, the cure for Empathy Deficit Disorder, I'm hoping you will "dare to be first" in supporting me today.

II.

A few words first about empathy and reason prior to the story of my remarkable discovery of Empathy Deficit Disorder, a feat sure to be honored with great renown. In the May 20, 2013, edition of the *New Yorker*, Paul Bloom wrote a concise (if not exactly Lincolnesque) essay called "The Baby in the Well." It's a critique of our ready rush to empathy as *the* answer to all the world's ills, including the ones we so often see in our work. The essay's title refers to a story I remember well, as will your parents. In 1987, a baby named Jessica McClure fell into a well somewhere in Texas. Bloom goes on to mention similar well-recalled events, from another child who in 1949 fell into some other well, to those without happy endings, such as the 2005 disappearance of a teenager named Natalee Holloway while vacationing in Aruba. "Why," he asks, "do people respond to these misfortunes and not to others?" Bloom—like many of you here, a student of psychology—reviews the works of his colleagues: "The psychologist Paul Slovic points out that, when Holloway disappeared, the story of her plight took up far more television time than the concurrent genocide in Darfur. Each day, more than 10 times the number of people who died in Hurricane Katrina die because of preventable diseases and more than 13 times as many perish from malnutrition."

Empathy, Bloom concludes, "has some unfortunate features—it is parochial, narrow-minded, and innumerate." As to how the term is innumerate, he makes (for those of you not leaving UD with a degree in applied mathematics) the following point: "The number of victims hardly matters—there's little psychological difference between hearing about the suffering of 5,000 and that of 500,000. Imagine reading that 2,000 people just died in an earthquake in a remote country, and then discovering that the actual number of deaths was 20,000. Do you now feel 10 times worse? To the extent that we recognize the numbers as significant, it's because of reason, not empathy." The essayist concludes as follows: "Our best hope for the future is not to get people to think of all humanity as family—that's impossible. It lies, instead, in an appreciation of the fact that, even if we don't empathize with distant strangers, their lives have the same value of the lives of those we love."

I went back and read the essay again yesterday, since I so often rely on empathy and work in such "remote" countries, including one not so remote from Delaware in which a recent earthquake took more than 200,000 lives. Bloom's tone may be grumpy—and I'm not saying that because he's a professor at Yale—but I get his point: empathy is not only innumerate but also an "unstable emotion," like pity or mercy or compassion. But can unstable emotions like empathy and compassion be transformed into something more enduring? Can a spark of empathy once ignited—however briefly, however tenuously—lead to reasoned decisions and to compassionate policies that might transform our world, including the precincts in which we live, into one in which there are fewer tragedies or less brutal echoes of them?

I think the answer to these questions is an emphatic *Yes*. To make my case, I offer you an improbable story of collective Empathy Deficit Disorder and of some of the steps taken to cure it. The story will take us back over three decades, and from the United States to Rwanda, where Partners In Health has worked for the better part of a decade.

Perhaps the story was improbable to me because I didn't know much of it until one week ago, when I read a new book by, of all people, Elton John. He's the promised rock star in this story. I knew that John had founded an important foundation, since it has supported Partners In Health's work in rural Haiti. But, to be honest, I didn't know how deeply and for how long he had been involved in reaching out directly to AIDS patients living in poverty in places like Atlanta, Georgia, or New York City, until I read his new book, *Love Is the Cure*, nor did I fully understand his foundation's work in places including Haiti, South Africa, and the Ukraine, to name just a few. My only excuse for not appreciating fully Elton John's engagement is a pretty lame one: between my father and my children, between "Crocodile Rock" and *The Lion King*, I'd experienced an excessive battering with his songs for much of my childhood and most of my adult years.

This story is about Mr. John's empathy and what he did to transform empathy into action and reason. It's about EDD and its diagnosis, often easy, and its cure, which is harder. Here's part of the story as he tells it. In 1985, the British rock star was thumbing through a magazine and read about an American boy born with hemophilia. The boy, who hailed from a small town in the Midwest, was in and out of the hospital throughout his childhood. Like so many afflicted with this disorder but with access to care, he relied on infusions of a clotting factor to stop a painful, potentially lethal, hemorrhage. As some of you will recall, U.S. supplies of Factor VIII, harvested from donated blood, were suddenly and widely contaminated with HIV, the virus that in 1984 was discovered to cause AIDS, which had been first described only three years previously. A huge fraction of hemophiliacs who relied on such treatments were subsequently discovered to be sick or infected.

This boy was one of them. His name was Ryan White. He was given six months to live. The year was 1984. The town was Kokomo, Indiana. Although Ryan's mother, who worked at the local General Motors plant, shared this hard news with her teenaged son, it was not Jeanne White's plan, in those first years of a frightening new epidemic, to broadcast the news widely. But a local paper ran a story disclosing her son's diagnosis. Soon the whole town knew. As if Ryan, sick with both hemophilia and AIDS, didn't have enough problems, he was soon shunned and mocked by his peers; his locker at school, vandalized. The grown-ups were even worse. After one grueling hospitalization, Ryan was prevented from returning to school, although the medical community was pretty confident, even then, that the disease could not be spread through casual contact. Even at his church, no one would shake Ryan's outstretched hand during the Rite of Peace. His mother and sister were also treated as pariahs. They were all threatened and worse. This was, of course, a stunning lack of both empathy and reason. It's a classic case, retrospectively diagnosed, of collective Empathy Deficit Disorder.

Ryan and his mother decided to sue the school, not so much to cure EDD as to return Ryan to his classroom. A local judge dismissed the Whites' lawsuit, instructing their lawyers that, if they had a gripe with the school superintendent's decision, they were welcome to take it up with the Indiana Department of Education. During his appeal, Ryan could only listen in to his classes, calling in each day from home.

Elton John describes what happened next.

> The appeals process that ensued was long, nasty and public, with Ryan, now 14 years old, at the center of it all. The local school board

and many parents of Ryan's schoolmates were vehemently opposed to him attending school. More than a hundred parents threatened to file a lawsuit if Ryan was allowed to return. In late November, the Indiana Department of Education ruled in Ryan's favor and ordered the school to open its doors to him, except then he was very sick. The local school board appealed, prolonging Ryan's absence from the classroom. Months later, a state board again ruled that Ryan should be allowed to attend school with the approval of a county health official.

With more than half the school year gone, Ryan was officially cleared to return to classes on February 21, 1986. The thrill of victory, though, was short-lived. On his first day back, he was pulled from the classroom and brought to court. A group of parents had filed an injunction to block his return, and the judge issued a restraining order against him. When the judge handed down his verdict, the room packed with parents began to cheer, while Ryan and Jeanne looked on, shocked and scared.*

---

* Elton John, *Love Is the Cure: On Life, Loss, and the End of AIDS* (New York: Little, Brown and Company, 2012).

At this point, even the least accomplished diagnostician will see, again, persistent unreason and further evidence of severe, chronic, collective EDD.

So why am I offering this story as an example of how empathy might be harnessed to reason and to long-lasting change? Because Ryan's story goes on, as does Mr. John's, in part because unstable emotions like empathy led to something better, more stable: "Like millions of people," John continues, "when I read about Ryan in that magazine . . . I was incensed. More than that, I was overcome with the desire to do something for him and his family. 'This situation is outrageous,' I thought. 'I've got to help these people.'"

Granted, the rock star didn't then have, he reports, a clue about what to do to help Ryan and his family. But he took that spark of fellow-feeling, which all of us can know, and made something of it.

During that very same year, 1986, I was a medical student at Harvard and interested in AIDS because I met, first in Haiti and later in Harvard teaching hospitals, young people dying of it. Like many of my classmates, I too was distressed about Ryan White's treatment. We were distressed about *all* those whose suffering, much of it caused by discrimination, was not then often addressed in magazines such as the one Mr. John had been reading when he first learned of Ryan's plight. As some of you will recall, AIDS was erroneously said to have originated in Haiti, and my first book, published over two decades ago, was in a sense about the relationship between AIDS and collective Empathy Deficit Disorder—even though I had not yet coined the phrase.

Moving from fear or outrage to reasoned action can be fueled by empathy. This empathic leap also occurred for Elton John and for many others, including AIDS activist groups; it continues to happen every day on campuses like UD. Ryan White became much more than a symbol or a cipher even before he died, at the age of eighteen, in 1990. His brave response to adversity, and that of other Americans who died of AIDS and also from neglect and scorn, led to something better. This happened because scientific and clinical research gave us, in the course of less than thirty years, decent treatment for AIDS. But didn't these three decades give us examples of decent treatment for neglect and scorn, too? Yes, it did, in part because Ryan's mother and many others, including heroic activists from ACT UP and others who "dare to be first," took their own unstable emotions and transformed them into pragmatic plans to help others similarly afflicted.

This unlikely coalition took its emotion and resolve and growing knowledge to Washington, to fight for new rules of the road. To return one last time to Mr. John's account: "In August 1990, only four months after Ryan's death, Congress passed the Ryan White Comprehensive AIDS Resources Emergency (CARE) Act in his honor . . .

Today, over 20 years later, Ryan's law provides more than $2 billion in AIDS treatment and prevention services each year to half a million Americans. The vast majority of those who receive assistance through the Ryan White CARE Act are low-income, uninsured people living with HIV/AIDS."*

I repeat: *low-income, uninsured* people. This describes neither a British rock star nor, at least technically, the son of a woman working for General Motors. Thus is empathy transformed into what some of us term "pragmatic solidarity." This sort of transformation, I announce here on Saturday, the twenty-fifth of May, is the cure for Empathy Deficit Disorder.

Today, in our clinical work in Boston, we often speak of some of our patients' social and medical needs as being met "by Ryan White funds." But it's easy to forget how outbreaks of EDD hurt, badly, the people most affected by AIDS. The great majority of them were not children, but grown-ups. Some of them, the ones who really did dare to be first, fought back with a brand of informed activism that changed how and with what tools we do much of our clinical work not only in Boston, but in places like Haiti and Rwanda and Lesotho. That's one of the reasons why Partners In Health is able to even *contemplate* how

---

* John, *Love Is the Cure.*

best to address the ranking health problems of the poor, whatever they might be, in the places we work. What if the list includes, as it often does, breast cancer? Major depressive disorder? Drug-resistant tuberculosis? Death during childbirth? Whenever people harness empathy, fight apathy, and seek to address the global pandemic of EDD, we learn how to build systems to fight discrimination and neglect and to deliver health care to those who need it most.

Ours is a nation still saddled with a big EDD problem, however. If you're poor and have AIDS in its nearby capital, EDD can be lethal: neglect is rarely benign and discrimination never is. But let me close with an improbably uplifting story because it's important to me that you know that the results of comprehensive efforts to treat EDD can be excellent and far-reaching *even when efforts to prevent it have already failed.* This is the story of one of the places that went up in flames in the midst of epidemic EDD. At the close of 1994, after a genocide that took up to a million lives, Rwanda lay in ruins. Many of its hospitals and clinics had been damaged or destroyed; others were simply abandoned; a large portion of the health workforce had been killed or was in refugee camps. These settlements, especially those within Rwanda, were thinned by cholera and other "camp epidemics" and by a rising tide of AIDS, tuberculosis, and malaria. Child mortality was the highest in the world; malnutrition was rampant. Many development experts were ready to write this small nation off as a lost cause, a failed state, a hopeless enterprise. There was some empathy, sure, but there was mostly horror and numbness and despair. This was a severe case of acute post-traumatic EDD, worsening the chronic EDD that had preceded it and indeed helped set the stage for the genocide.

Cut to nineteen years later, as you graduate from UD. Today, Rwanda is the only country in sub-Saharan Africa on track to meet, by 2015, each of the health-related Millennium Development Goals that almost all the world's countries agreed upon fifteen years ago. More than 93 percent of Rwandan infants are inoculated against eleven vaccine-preventable illnesses. Over the past decade, death during childbirth has declined by more than 60 percent. Deaths attributed to AIDS, tuberculosis, and malaria have dropped even more steeply, as have all deaths registered among children under five. Rwanda is one of only two countries on the continent to achieve the goal of universal access to AIDS therapy; the other is far wealthier Botswana. There's still a long way to go. *But these are some of the steepest declines in mortality ever documented, anywhere and at any time in recorded history.*

If that's not a big-time reversal of fortune, I don't know what is. This has come to pass for many reasons and with the help of many partners; it has come to pass because of good leadership in Rwanda and sound policies in development, as in public health and in clinical medicine. But most of all, I will argue here, it has come to pass because Empathy Deficit Disorder was addressed within and without Rwanda's borders. After all, most of this improvement has occurred among the poor and in the country's *rural* reaches, traditionally neglected in all settings in which epidemic EDD is registered, which is to say just about everywhere.

But some of this improvement in Rwanda has also come to pass because the global pandemic of EDD is being diagnosed and addressed in our own country. The United States is far and away the largest single funder of AIDS treatment programs in Africa. The same is true of malaria and many other health problems. And there's little doubt that many Americans, even in places like Ryan White's hometown in Indiana, now support efforts to build up an empathy surplus and to help build reasoned programs that can save lives, improve health, and mitigate the impact of future outbreaks of EDD. For this, I thank you as both a doctor and an American.

III.

I end on this upbeat note because my diagnostic research on the student body here reveals only low rates of EDD at UD. This is not only because your mascots are called "the Fightin' Blue Hens." This would seem to call for pity more than empathy. I'm sure such hens are worthy, and probably even blue, but poultry of any sort so rarely inspire the sort of fear you want on a football field.

But he digresses, your president and deans and parents are thinking.

Close by joining me in a thought exercise. *Contemplate* the enormity of the challenges before our nation and our species and our planet, from climate change and unfettered population growth to economic recessions triggered by mind-bogglingly unsound business practices and on to violence and war. *Remember* the story of Ryan White, or that of the millions who died before there was a Ryan White CARE Act or a Global Fund to Fight AIDS, Tuberculosis and Malaria, or the U.S. programs with similar, global reach. *Remember* the story of Rwanda's spectacular turnaround.

Now look around you. You are graduating from faculties with names like Earth, Ocean, and Environment. Engineering. Health Science. And within these schools, think of the degrees awarded here. Human Development and Family Studies. Nursing. Urban Affairs and Public Policy. Psychology. The list goes on, as it should, since you've had since 1743 to get UD up and running.

You can be the cure for EDD in its chronic and acute forms. You can be the folks who address local outbreaks of EDD and also the global pandemic, which has affected people in every single nation on this fragile and crowded planet. Indeed, ours is a world that requires nothing less than linking empathy and compassion to reasoned plans that harness them to meaningful action. I don't think anyone sitting out there, or up here, believes for a minute that humanity doesn't have a future. The UD students I met with last night and this morning remind me of the talent and smarts and goodwill of the next generation. But even our short-term survival calls for deliberation and calculation and expertise. These will not be marshaled in adequate quantities nor for the public good unless we address the global pandemic of Empathy Deficit Disorder. And that, dear Class of 2013, is well within our grasp.

Thank you for hearing me out, oh empaths of UD! Congratulations to all of you, to your loved ones, and to that much larger group that might benefit from empathy and compassion transformed into solidarity and beneficent action.

NOT FOR PROFIT

Martha Nussbaum

CONNECTICUT COLLEGE, 2009

ON THIS JOYFUL DAY, we are here to celebrate a wonderful group of young people who have achieved so much, graduating from one of the premier liberal arts colleges in the United States, and who face exciting prospects for the future. The type of liberal education you have received, however, is under assault all over the world in our time of economic anxiety, as all nations compete to keep or increase their share in the global market. All over the world, radical changes are occurring in what democratic societies teach both children and young adults, and these changes have not been well considered. Thirsty for economic gain, nations, and their systems of education, are heedlessly discarding forms of learning that are crucial to the health of democracy.

What are these radical changes? The humanities and the arts, the core of our idea of "liberal arts education," are being downsized and downgraded. Seen as useless frills, at a time when nations must cut away all useless things in order to stay competitive in the global market, they are rapidly losing their place in curricula, and in the minds and hearts of parents and children. Indeed, what we might call the humanistic aspect of science and social science— the imaginative, creative aspect and the aspect of rigorous critical thought—are also losing ground, as nations prefer to pursue short-term profit by emphasizing useful, highly applied skills, suited to short-term profit making.

The U.S. has resisted these changes better than many nations, thanks to our time-honored tradition of liberal education at the college level, which sends curricular and pedagogical signals to schools as well. We, too, however, are in grave danger of going down the road toward a narrow profit-focused education. Increasingly, in news reports and op-eds, we read of a decline in the humanities, of programs in music, art, and theater pared away at the high school level, of humanities curricula being downsized at the college level.

Consider, too, the Spellings Report on the state of higher education in the U.S., released in 2006 by the U.S. Department of Education under the leadership of

Bush administration secretary of education Margaret Spellings. Called *A Test of Leadership: Charting the Future of U.S. Higher Education*,* this report contained a valuable critique of unequal access to higher education. When it

What does a liberal education contribute to the health of democracy?

came to subject matter, however, it focused entirely on education for national economic gain. It concerned itself with perceived deficiencies in science, technology, and engineering—not even basic scientific research in these areas, but only highly applied learning, learning that can quickly generate profit-making strategies. The humanities, the arts, and critical thinking, so important for decent global citizenship, were basically absent. By omitting them, the report strongly suggested that it would be perfectly all right if these abilities were allowed to wither away, in favor of more useful disciplines.

---

* *A Test of Leadership: Charting the Future of U.S. Higher Education*, available online. A valuable counterreport is *College Learning for the New Global Century*, issued by the National Leadership Council for Liberal Education and America's Promise (LEAP), a group organized by the Association of American Colleges and Universities (Washington, D.C., 2007), with whose recommendations I am largely in agreement (not surprisingly, in that I participated in drafting it).

Why should we care? All of you have had a liberal education, and President Higdon often says to you, "A liberal arts education is the best preparation for life and career." But why? What difference would it really make if Connecticut College scrapped its liberal arts focus in favor of technological and preprofessional studies?

We could go in a number of directions from here, since a liberal arts education does many things. It is a preparation for life, and I think you will appreciate more and more, as life goes on, the expansion of your mind and heart that your education here has made possible. I've so often met people in all walks of life—law, engineering, business—who feel that their ability to enjoy life, to think about other people and themselves, and to understand the world around them was decisively affected by the quality of their own undergraduate liberal arts education. We could also talk about business, since leading business educators have recently been placing great emphasis on the need for liberal arts education as a part of what keeps our business culture healthy and dynamic. They stress particularly the importance of the humanities in developing the imagination, and the importance of critical thinking in producing a business culture that is not simply a culture of yes-people: both fraud and failure often emerge from a situation in which people are unwilling or unable to raise a critical voice.

But I want to talk today about the role of liberal education in producing democratic citizens, the sort of citizen who can keep democracy alive and realize its promise. So: What does a liberal education that contains a substantial contribution from the humanities and the arts contribute to the health of democracy?

Three capacities, above all, are essential to the survival and progress of democracy in today's complicated world. They are all, I believe, built into the structure of education at Connecticut College and other similar liberal arts colleges. First is the capacity for critical examination of oneself and one's traditions—for living what, following Socrates, we may call "the examined life." This means a life that accepts no belief as authoritative simply because it has been handed down by tradition or become familiar through habit, a life that questions all beliefs and accepts only those that survive reason's demand for consistency and for justification. Training this capacity requires developing the capacity to reason logically, to test what one reads or says for consistency of reasoning, correctness of fact, and accuracy of judgment. Testing of this sort frequently produces challenges to tradition, as Socrates knew well when he defended himself against the charge of "corrupting the young." But he defended his activity on the grounds that democracy needs citizens who can think for themselves rather than simply deferring to authority, who can reason together about their choices rather than just trading claims and counterclaims. Like a gadfly on the back of a noble but sluggish horse, he said, he was waking democracy up so that it could conduct its business in a more reflective and reasonable way.

Our American democracy, like ancient Athens, is prone to hasty and sloppy reasoning, and to the substitution of invective for real deliberation. With the decline in newspapers and the increasing influence of an impoverished talk-radio culture of sound bites, we need Socrates in the classroom more urgently than ever. Critical argument gives people a way of being responsible: when politicians bring simplistic rhetoric their way, they won't just accept it or reject it on the basis of a prior ideological commitment; they will investigate and argue, thinking for themselves, and learning to understand themselves. And when argument, not mere partisan feeling, takes the lead, people will also be able to interact with one another in a more reasonable way. Instead of seeing political disputes as occasions to score points for their own side, and ultimately to win a victory over the opposition, they will probe, investigate; they will learn where the other person's argument shares common ground with their own; all this conduces to respect and understanding.

Critical thinking can be found in many parts of the education you have had at Connecticut, but perhaps it is especially found in Area 4, Critical Studies in Literature and the Arts, and in Area 6, Philosophical and Religious Studies—two of the areas of study that are most threatened in the current world rush to profit.

Responsible democratic citizens who cultivate their humanity need, further, an ability to see themselves as not simply citizens of some

Good citizenship requires that we challenge our imaginative capacity.

local region or group, but also, and above all, as human beings bound to all other human beings by ties of recognition and concern. All modern democracies are inescapably plural. As citizens within each nation we are frequently called upon to make decisions that require some understanding of racial and ethnic and religious groups in that nation, and of the situation of its women and its sexual minorities. As citizens we are also increasingly called upon to understand how issues such as agriculture, human rights, climate change, business and industry, and, of course, violence and terrorism are generating discussions that bring people together from many different nations. This must happen more and more, if effective solutions to pressing human problems are to be found. But these connections often take, today, a very thin form: the global market, which sees human lives as instruments for gain. If institutions of higher education do not build a richer network of human connections, it is likely that our dealings with one another will be mediated by the impoverished norms of market exchange and profit making. And these impoverished norms do not help, to put it mildly, if what we want is a world of peace, where people will be able to live fruitful, cooperative lives.

Becoming good citizens in a complex interlocking world involves understanding the ways in which common needs and aims are differently realized in different circumstances. This requires a great deal of knowledge that American college students rarely got in previous eras—knowledge of non-Western cultures, and also of minorities within their own, of differences of gender and sexuality. History and the other social sciences are key disciplines here, and they need to be taught, as they are in an excellent liberal arts college, with an emphasis on the independent thinking of the student, who learns to evaluate evidence, to think about the relationship between history and her own time, and to think critically about different accounts of concepts such as economic well-being and global development.

The study of a foreign language is an extremely valuable part of this group of abilities, since there is no better way to understand cultural difference than to see how another society has cut up the world in subtly different ways, how any translation is always an interpretation and approximation. So I applaud your language requirement: even if the language you have studied is that of a relatively familiar culture, it has given you an irreplaceable training for navigating in a world of many cultures.

But citizens cannot think well on the basis of factual knowledge alone. The third ability of the citizen, closely related to the first two, can be called the narrative imagination. We all are born with a basic capacity to see the world from another person's point of view. That capacity, which we share with a number of other animal species, is a part of our biological heritage. This capacity, however, needs development, and it particularly needs development in areas in which our society has created sharp separations between groups. We know that human beings are all too capable of what psychologist Robert Jay Lifton, in his powerful book *The Nazi Doctors*, calls "splitting": that is, we can live lives rich in empathy with our own group, recognizing the humanity of its members, while denying humanity to other groups and people. Good citizenship requires that we challenge our imaginative capacity, learning what the world looks like from the point of view of groups we typically try not to see. Ralph Ellison, in a later essay about his great novel *Invisible Man*, wrote that a novel such as his could be "a raft of perception, hope, and entertainment" on which American culture could "negotiate the snags and whirlpools" that stand between us and our democratic ideal. His novel, of course, takes the "inner eyes" of the white reader as its theme and its target. The hero is invisible to white society, but he tells us that this invisibility is an imaginative and educational failing on their part, not a biological accident on his. This ability is cultivated, above all, by courses in the arts and humanities. And I think it is in some ways the most essential of all, if we are to work toward a world in which we see distant lives as spacious and deep, rather than simply as occasions for enrichment.

The imagination of humanness, we might call it. And this ability is cultivated not only by the study of literature, but also by music, fine arts, dance, and the other creative arts—a reason why I am so impressed with your decision to give the arts a separate place in your liberal education requirements.

Today, in elementary and high schools all over America, the arts are being slashed away, since they look like useless frills that don't help America make money. All too few colleges and universities send the strong signal of respect for them that your own does, and many are even downsizing or eliminating the arts themselves. Literature is still hanging in there, because of its core role in many general education curricula, but wait twenty years and this too may be a thing of the past. The Indian poet, philosopher, and educator Rabindranath Tagore, builder of an experimental school and a liberal arts university, observed already in 1917 that the demands of the global economy threatened the eclipse of abilities that were crucial for a world of justice and peace.

[H]istory has come to a stage when the moral
man, the complete man, is more and more giving way, almost without knowing it, to make
room for the . . . commercial man, the man
of limited purpose. This process, aided by
the wonderful progress in science, is assum-
ing gigantic proportion and power, causing
the upset of man's moral balance, obscuring
his human side under the shadow of soul-less
organization.*

In twenty years, the world may remember the sort of
education you have received as a distant memory. If that
is the way the future unfolds, the world will be a scary
place to live in. What will we have, if these trends continue? Nations of technically trained people who don't
know how to criticize authority, useful profit makers with
obtuse imaginations. As Tagore observed, a suicide of the
soul. What could be more frightening than that? In my
study of the Indian state of Gujarat, which has for a particularly long time gone down this road, with no critical
thinking or imagining in the public schools and a con-
certed focus on technical ability, one can see clearly how

---

* Tagore, *Nationalism*, 1917.

a band of docile technicians can be welded into a murderous force to enact the most horrendously racist and antidemocratic policies.

But the future does not have to unfold this way. It is in our hands, and, especially, in the hands of all of you, who have had this sort of education—you know its value, and will come to know it more as the years go on. What you can do is to keep institutions like Connecticut College strong; lobby with your state and national representatives for more attention to the humanities and the arts, which even President Obama seems bent on neglecting. Above all, just talk a lot about what matters to you. Spread the word that what happens on this campus is not useless, but crucially relevant to the future of democracy in the nation and the world.

Democracies have great rational and imaginative powers. They also are prone to some serious flaws in reasoning, to parochialism, haste, sloppiness, selfishness. Education based mainly on profitability in the global market magnifies these deficiencies, producing a greedy obtuseness and a technically trained docility that threaten the very life of democracy itself, and that certainly impede the creation of a decent world culture. If the real clash of civilizations is, as I believe, a clash within the individual soul, as greed and narcissism contend against respect and love, all modern societies are rapidly losing the battle, as they feed the forces that lead to violence and dehumanization and fail to feed the forces that lead to cultures of equality and respect. If we do not insist on the crucial importance of the humanities and the arts, they will drop away, because they don't make money. They only do what is much more precious than that, make a world that is worth living in, people who are able to see other human beings as equals, and nations that are able to overcome fear and suspicion in favor of sympathetic and reasoned debate.

Congratulations. May you live happy and productive lives in our complicated world, taking your education with you and fighting to keep it alive for others.

Know Your History

Oliver Stone

UNIVERSITY OF CALIFORNIA, LOS ANGELES,* 2009

I HAD A TOUGH TIME preparing these remarks because I don't want to bore you. I've been through enough of these types of speeches when I was young that frankly I don't remember anything anybody ever said. I remember the face of the speaker, the mood, the attitude, but I don't remember what was said, and what can I say today that can give you the necessary courage you will need? Nor am I sure I'd like to be on the other side of this podium right now. They say you're facing a pretty bad job

---

* This speech was delivered to the 2009 graduating class of the UCLA School of Theater, Film and Television.

market, economic devastation, climate change, two wars
in Afghanistan and Iraq, a serious health cost crisis. And,
of course, the greatest war of all—the one that George W.
Bush declared and called the War on Terror.

It is clear this is being pictured to us as a time of great
fear. We have all looked inside ourselves, and tried to remember when we felt similar feelings. When I was your
age there was Vietnam. There were the Kennedy assas-
sinations, and there was Martin Luther King Jr., turbu-
lence, riots in cities—and yes, there were also no jobs in
1971 in film and certainly not in the television business.
The government felt like it was losing control. There
were all these kids walkin' around smokin' dope and
looking weird and making all kinds of dissident music
with strange new lyrics. So people were really scared and
most, as a result, voted for the law and order candidate.
The tyrant, Richard Nixon. The rest followed as does
the night the day. As did Reagan. As did Bush. Each the
father to the son. Each of the three an angry backlash to
a perceived violation—or one could call it fear.

Fear is a distorting and powerful emotion. Young or
old, we've all experienced it. It's a beast—the 600 pound
gorilla we face in the room every day. Telling us you
can't, you musn't, stop! This beast gets right in front of
you and it's a loud beast; it doesn't actually touch us, but
it yells and turns red and makes faces until we get crazy
in our heads. Some of us get scared, back down, and run.

But, the truth is, fear cannot actually make you do what it wants. You can do what it tells you, or you can say, "Hey fear, I appreciate what you're trying to tell me and I understand there's danger here, but now you've said

Remember the past, because without memory there is only the dictatorship of now.

what you have to say. So please now leave me alone—go away. Come back tomorrow. And I'll listen again to what you've gotta say." Then watch the look on fear's face— hold that look. Breathe through it. And you know what— the beast may just stop yelling and back down, because he sees that you're not gonna change and you're not going to do what he wants you to do. And he gets tired of yelling. And tomorrow when he comes back, he just might be a little bit smaller. And the next day. And the next. Shrink the bastard. Eventually you might make fear, if not a close buddy, maybe an ally. As Alexander said to his troops on the eve of battle, "Conquer your fear and you will conquer death."

Our media generally tries to create a common denominator of thought that straitjackets us. This is this, that's that, and it's because of this and because of that. Sometimes in the middle of all of that there are some facts, and that's why we read the media, because we try to see through the smoke to the fire. But, generally, they're saying stuff that's pessimistic. They're selling bad news. After all, their reasoning goes, they gotta make a buck and if I don't, the other guy's going to do it. On television it's murder, disease, deaths, crises, and failure every minute.

Whether you've realized it or not, and maybe some of you have not traveled outside the country, they frame most every argument like it's America against the world and we have enemies everywhere. Whether it be tiny Cuba, bristling Venezuela, or the biggies like Russia and China, or tomorrow India, or tomorrow Pakistan, or tomorrow Africa, or tomorrow Canada, or tomorrow Mexico, or tomorrow and tomorrow and tomorrow. Creeps out this petty pace from year to year until the end of recorded time. What emerges from this daily persuasion is unfortunately an ethnocentric, egocentric American point of view in our lifetime. And the resulting calls for reaction. And, unfortunately, many of us pay that price as we get swept up in the waves of history created and enforced by media, and common misperception. As you get older some of you may realize that life is always filled with problems, but when we act or react childishly to them, as if they're bigger than they are, which is the media's way, it's generally because we believe that we are the only ones who are having this problem, when we are not.

Not too long ago in around 1900 all these great Western empires were congratulating themselves about the greatness of Western civilization, partly because they controlled, through their colonies, almost the entire world's surface and its resources. Though an incredible 10 to 12 million natives were killed in the Belgian Congo, they told us the world was civilized—electricity, industry, money, federal reserve boards, free trade, tariffs, British Empire, maritime duties—and then they all marched as one into one of the most brutal and ugliest wars of all time: World War I, fought with gas, chemical agents, horrifying bombs. And it marked the end of the European empires.

Chaos resulted, the West rescrambled the territories, and within twenty years was at war again, a yet even bloodier war called World War II. From that grew more and more mythologies and deceptions that I grew up with. Lies, lies, lies, that's what you're going to get as you get older. In my lifetime I've been through fighting communism from the 1940s to the 1990s. We killed so many. We subverted so many countries in the name of freedom and democracy, and we bloated ourselves in numerous wars throughout the planet. America became the new empire, and more important became a war-making and war-loving country. In the very same way we hone the art of money, as another weapon of mass destruction.

And by 2000, a hundred years after 1900, if some of you remember correctly not too long ago—you were twelve, thirteen—there was an amazing arrogance in the

American establishment and media about our dominant role in the world, and how everyone now was going to follow the American model. There was going to be neoliberal economics and globalization. With the Soviet empire now collapsed, it was American triumphalism at its worst. And George Bush, to me, historically will represent the overweening pride, and shallowness, and stupidity of that moment in 2000 when he callously stole this election. Well, anybody who knows history could see this coming, and the last eight years have certainly lived up to it. A nightmare beyond most conceivable proportions to a person who grew up in the sixties and seventies, whose damage will be known in the coming years to you. We have lost our image as a country that believes in immigration, in change, and idealisms, and [become] one that has come to oppress those who seek change in their own countries. But is it the worst of times? I don't know. I think it's always been tough. Maybe a few years here and there of relative peace, but peace is not an easy thing to achieve. Peace is truly the result of struggle. And war is the result of the failure of a struggling peace.

Most important, it is the struggle inside yourself that will make your peace, and it is up to you. I'm not the first one to say that peace can only begin once you have come to grips with your own aggressiveness, but I do believe it. We cannot do anything unless we change ourselves. And that is often the hardest of all. When they ask you, "Are you having a good day? It's okay. Are you having a bad day? That's okay, too." Good day, bad day—same thing. "I'm okay." That's the point—take the good, the bad, the neutral, stir, mix and live in equanimity and balance. For this you got an education. Believe it or not that is probably the most important thing you can get here—a process by which you can develop and discipline your mind. The challenge of growing up is learning to live with setbacks and challenges. You've learned about film. You've learned about the history of it, its traditions, but the real point of film is to shape your mind in the same way that history, sociology, economics, mathematics, and the sciences shape your mind—to teach you how to think. To shape your mind so that you can take the same world that exists for all these sciences and arts, and give back to it, contribute to it, nurture it, and create civilization with film. Fight everything that's toxic in this civilization. Read, especially film students. I urge you to read history and remember the past, because without memory there is only the dictatorship of now. The panic of now. The panic of an immature president like George W. Bush, overreacting to the terrorist acts of 9/11, and saying we've got to fight back. It's us against them. We're the deciders and the world is a free fire zone and our phones/our privacy/our rights are all subject to the rules of the state. This is the beast of fear yelling in your face—"What are you gonna do! You gotta do something! Revenge! Bomb!

Kill! Don't be a softy! Act tough!" That is always going
to happen to you. Your whole life is going to be these vig-
ilante mobs with this desire for revenge and blood. There
are even Hollywood filmmakers doing very well, getting
Pentagon cooperation, making movies promoting technology. Military technology that is awesome and makes
you want to kill, makes you want to fight, makes you want
to use it! This is not what you came to school for.

And there's always another terrorist, there's always another Dick Cheney around the corner with another version of a nightmare. It will never go away. Terror is having
this fear of depression, communism, drugs, homosexuality, poverty, and generally anything. But neither terror, nor drugs, nor poverty, nor communism, nor social
change, nor equality, nor abortion, nor homosexuality, nor
any of these demands for change and freedom will ever
cease. That's the reality of the world. And there will always be those who [go] along with change, and there are
those who resist change. It seems it always breaks down
to those two categories at the end of the day. History,
strewn with corpses, can attest to that. They yell their
soundless warnings, and yet we never hear, watching a
younger generation march off to new wars with approving
smiles. Renders an old man sad. What power do we really
have to alter any landscape but our own?

Your responsibility here as graduating students is, I repeat, to civilization, to read history, to know humanity,

and above all to remember the past. I repeat again, because "repetition works"—but without memory there is only the dictatorship of now.

The knowledge of history will teach you that empires cannot succeed with physical or economic force alone. But only in the realm of the spirit. Your mind is the asset which you have appreciated while you were here. And if it is open it will continue to grow through your life. It is your concentration that has to hold up in the face of adversity. Water your mind like a garden—a little sun, a little rain, a little fertilizer, some insects, some adversity, a little of this, a little of that, but never damage your garden with too much of this or too much of that. Your mind is a beautiful thing. Strong and not fragile, it can take excess and abuse, but only so much. Fear, at first, might be your taskmaster, but in the end it may well be your friend. And your friends in life may betray you, and your enemies may become your best teachers. Accept the paradox. Don't judge, until you know. And then when you know, you know. Try everything. And don't forget to read history, as much of it as you can get.

Jim Morrison of the Doors may not have made it out of UCLA Film School, but don't be discouraged. He died too young, but he lived life like a flower with his head in the breeze. Stay open.

And my best advice for those of you going out into the crazy, exciting world—don't fall in love right away. Don't get married. Get a backpack. A ticket to nowhere. Take a year off. Travel your ass off. Learn everything you can. Listen to the wind. It may cost you money not to work. But that year off is money. Time and experience is what will make your life rich. It's not going to make much difference in the end if you take your first job at twenty-one or twenty-four, as long as you grow, grow well.

So good-bye, good luck, and go out there no matter what happens—good day okay, bad day okay. Feel good about your effort and try to keep that smile on your face.

THE EARTH IS HIRING

Paul Hawken

UNIVERSITY OF PORTLAND, 2009

WHEN I WAS INVITED to give this speech, I was asked if I could give a simple short talk that was "direct, naked, taut, honest, passionate, lean, shivering, startling, and graceful." No pressure there. Let's begin with the startling part. Class of 2009: you are going to have to figure out what it means to be a human being on earth at a time when every living system is declining, and the rate of decline is accelerating. Kind of a mind-boggling situation . . . but not one peer-reviewed paper published in the last thirty years can refute that statement. Basically, civilization needs a new operating system, you are the programmers, and we need it within a few decades.

This planet came with a set of instructions, but we seem to have misplaced them. Important rules like don't poison the water, soil, or air; don't let the earth get over-crowded; and don't touch the thermostat have been broken. Buckminster Fuller said that spaceship earth was so ingeniously designed that no one has a clue that we are on one, flying through the universe at a million miles per hour, with no need for seat belts, lots of room in coach, and really good food—but all that is changing.

There is invisible writing on the back of the diploma you will receive, and in case you didn't bring lemon juice to decode it, I can tell you what it says: You Are Brilliant, and the Earth Is Hiring. The earth couldn't afford to send recruiters or limos to your school. It sent you rain, sunsets, ripe cherries, night-blooming jasmine, and that unbelievably cute person you are dating. Take the hint. And here's the deal: Forget that this task of planet saving is not possible in the time required. Don't be put off by people who know what is not possible. Do what needs to be done, and check to see if it was impossible only after you are done.

When asked if I am pessimistic or optimistic about the future, my answer is always the same: If you look at the science about what is happening on earth and aren't pessimistic, you don't understand the data. But if you meet the people who are working to restore this earth and the lives of the poor, and you aren't optimistic, you haven't got a pulse. What I see everywhere in the world are ordinary people willing to confront despair, power, and incalculable odds in order to restore some semblance of grace, justice, and beauty to this world. The poet Adrienne Rich wrote, "So much has been de-

Civilization needs a new operating system, you are the programmers, and we need it within a few decades.

stroyed I have cast my lot with those who, age after age, perversely, with no extraordinary power, reconstitute the world." There could be no better description. Humanity is coalescing. It is reconstituting the world, and the action is taking place in schoolrooms, farms, jungles, villages, campuses, companies, refugee camps, deserts, fisheries, and slums.

You join a multitude of caring people. No one knows how many groups and organizations are working on the most salient issues of our day: climate change, poverty, deforestation, peace, water, hunger, conservation, human rights, and more. This is the largest movement the world has ever seen. Rather than control, it seeks connection. Rather than dominance, it strives to disperse concentrations of power. Like Mercy Corps, it works behind the scenes and gets the job done. Large as it is, no one knows the true size of this movement. It provides hope, support, and meaning to billions of people in the world. Its clout resides in idea, not in force. It is made up of teachers, children, peasants, businesspeople, rappers, organic farmers, nuns, artists, government workers, fisherfolk, engineers, students, incorrigible writers, weeping Muslims, concerned mothers, poets, doctors without borders, grieving Christians, street musicians, the president of the United States of America, and, as the writer David James Duncan would say, the Creator, the One who loves us all in such a huge way.

There is a rabbinical teaching that says if the world is ending and the Messiah arrives, first plant a tree, and then see if the story is true. Inspiration is not garnered from the litanies of what may befall us; it resides in humanity's willingness to restore, redress, reform, rebuild, recover, reimagine, and reconsider. Consider moving away from the profane, toward a deep sense of connectedness to the living world.

Millions of people are working on behalf of strangers, even if the evening news is usually about the death of strangers. This kindness of strangers has religious, even mythic origins, and very specific eighteenth-century roots. Abolitionists were the first people to create a national and global movement to defend the rights of those they did not know. Until that time, no group had filed a grievance except on behalf of itself. The founders of this movement were largely unknown—Granville Clark,

Thomas Clarkson, Josiah Wedgwood—and their goal was ridiculous on the face of it. At that time three out of four people in the world were enslaved. Enslaving each other was what human beings had done for ages. And the abolitionist movement was greeted with incredulity. Conservative spokesmen ridiculed the abolitionists as liberals, progressives, do-gooders, meddlers, and activists. They were told they would ruin the economy and drive England into poverty. But for the first time in history a group of people organized themselves to help people they would never know, from whom they would never receive direct or indirect benefit. And today tens of millions of people do this every day. It is called the world of nonprofits, civil society, schools, social entrepreneurship, nongovernmental organizations, and companies who place social and environmental justice at the top of their strategic goals. The scope and scale of this effort is unparalleled in history.

The living world is not "out there" somewhere, but in your heart. What do we know about life? In the words of biologist Janine Benyus, life creates the conditions that are conducive to life. I can think of no better motto for a future economy. We have tens of thousands of abandoned homes without people and tens of thousands of abandoned people without homes. We have failed bankers advising failed regulators on how to save failed assets. We are the only species on the planet without full

employment. Brilliant. We have an economy that tells us
that it is cheaper to destroy earth in real time rather than
renew, restore, and sustain it. You can print money to bail
out a bank but you can't print life to bail out a planet. At
present we are stealing the future, selling it in the present, and calling it gross domestic product. We can just as
easily have an economy that is based on healing the future instead of stealing it. We can either create assets for
the future or take the assets of the future. One is called
restoration and the other exploitation. And whenever we
exploit the earth we exploit people and cause untold suffering. Working for the earth is not a way to get rich; it is
a way to be rich.

The first living cell came into being nearly 40 million
centuries ago, and its direct descendants are in all of our
bloodstreams. Literally, you are breathing molecules this
very second that were inhaled by Moses, Mother Teresa,
and Bono. We are vastly interconnected. Our fates are
inseparable. We are here because the dream of every cell
is to become two cells. And dreams come true. In each
of you are one quadrillion cells, 90 percent of which are
not human cells. Your body is a community, and without
those other microorganisms you would perish in hours.
Each human cell has 400 billion molecules conducting
millions of processes between trillions of atoms. The
total cellular activity in one human body is staggering:
one septillion actions at any one moment, a one with

twenty-four zeros after it. In a millisecond, our body has undergone ten times more processes than there are stars in the universe, which is exactly what Charles Darwin foretold when he said science would discover that each living creature was a "little universe, formed of a host of self-propagating organisms, inconceivably minute and as numerous as the stars of heaven."

So I have two questions for you all. First, can you feel your body? Stop for a moment. Feel your body. One septillion activities going on simultaneously, and your body does this so well you are free to ignore it, and wonder instead when this speech will end. You can feel it. It is called life. This is who you are. Second question: Who is in charge of your body? Who is managing those molecules? Hopefully not a political party. Life is creating the conditions that are conducive to life inside you, just as in all of nature. Our innate nature is to create the conditions that arc conducive to life. What I want you to imagine is that collectively humanity is evincing a deep, innate wisdom in coming together to heal the wounds and insults of the past.

Ralph Waldo Emerson once asked what we would do if the stars only came out once every thousand years. No one would sleep that night, of course. The world would create new religions overnight. We would be ecstatic, delirious, made rapturous by the glory of God. Instead, the stars come out every night and we watch television.

This extraordinary time when we are globally aware of each other and the multiple dangers that threaten civilization has never happened, not in a thousand years, not in ten thousand years. Each of us is as complex and beautiful as all the stars in the universe. We have done great things and we have gone way off course in terms of honoring creation. You are graduating to the most amazing, stupefying challenge ever bequeathed to any generation. The generations before you failed. They didn't stay up all night. They got distracted and lost sight of the fact that life is a miracle every moment of your existence. Nature beckons you to be on her side. You couldn't ask for a better boss. The most unrealistic person in the world is the cynic, not the dreamer. Hope only makes sense when it doesn't make sense to be hopeful. This is your century. Take it and run as if your life depends on it.

MAKE THIS WORLD A BETTER PLACE

Isabel Wilkerson

BATES COLLEGE, 2014

I HAVE ONLY FIFTEEN MINUTES, and fifteen minutes is not really enough time to say all that I wish I could say. It took me fifteen years—I brought a copy of this book I spent all this time on; this is my copy, it's all worn—to write the book that got me to this point, and it took so long that I often say that if this book were a human being, it would be in high school and dating, that's how long it took me to write this.

So, for me, fifteen minutes is not a lot of time. But I want to speak with you today about courage, about the courage that it took to create your alma mater, the courage that it took to bring our country into the modern era, and the courage that I know is within you as you leave this campus.

We are in a crisis in our country.

The world that you are entering is one of unimagined opportunity but also a world in peril, and it needs you, the Class of 2014, so very urgently. We are in a crisis in our country: a crisis of identity, a crisis of fairness, a crisis of who is seen as deserving and who is not, a crisis of who is American, or who is seen as American, and what it means to be American and what America should be and can be. And a crisis of what we should do about our tangled inheritance, what we should do about the sins of the past and the injustices of the present.

One reason for all of these crises is that we do not know where we have come from; we do not truly know the cost in human lives and in human blood that it took to create the country that we live in and the fruits that we enjoy. We do not truly know how we came to this moment, and the origins of the divisions of the tribe and caste that plague and handicap us to this day.

This year, the year of your graduation, is a milestone not just for you but for our country. Look at what has happened in the last fifty or sixty years. When your grandparents (and for some of you, when your parents) were born, it was actually against the law for a black person and a white person to merely play checkers together in Birmingham. You could go to jail if you were caught playing checkers with a person of a different race.

The very word of God was segregated.

It was against the law for a black person to take out a library book in Mississippi; in living

> *You have the courage within you to do wondrous things, miracles even.*

memory, throughout the South, there was actually a black Bible and an altogether separate white Bible to swear to tell the truth on in court. The very word of God was segregated. Throughout the South, black people were publicly executed for trying to vote and white people killed for trying to help them.

We are now on the eve of a watershed moment in that national struggle. Next month, it will be exactly fifty years since three young men your age—James Chaney, twenty-one, Andrew Goodman, twenty, and Michael Schwerner, twenty-four—were abducted and killed by a mob of eighteen men in Neshoba County, Mississippi, merely for trying to register African Americans, putatively free American citizens, to vote. It took forty years for anyone to be brought to justice in that case, and most of the perpetrators never spent a day in jail.

It was the national outrage over their deaths, combined with the courage of thousands of young protesters of all races, that helped propel the Civil Rights Act of 1964, outlawing discrimination in employment and in public spaces, along with the Voting Rights Act of 1965, protecting a citizen's right to vote. Which means that, if you know someone born before 1965, you know someone who was not born in a democracy. Think about that. Because until that time, millions of American citizens were prohibited from voting.

And yet, in the time since you have been in college, in four short years, many of these advances have been dismantled.

The Voting Rights Act, signed after the sorrow of Chaney, Goodman, and Schwerner, has been gutted. And we have gone from the triumph of the 1960s when the country became a true democracy—by opening doors for women, for black people, for non-European immigrants, and for the disabled—to the now coarser, harsher public discourse of today, with one racially charged case after another making headlines, with crude racial outbursts by public figures, and with worsening disparities between blacks and whites in every sphere of life, from education to employment to housing and income to incarceration rates, all of them deep scars of ancient wounds that have not been confronted, much less healed.

These ancient wounds are our inheritance to face up to, to repair, and to learn from. The wounds come from the divisions, fears, and hatreds that created 246 years of enslavement of one set of people by another. That means twelve generations. These divisions led the country to civil war. They led to a hundred years of legal subjugation of one set of people by another well into the twentieth century and unspeakable violence and heartbreak for millions of people still alive today. These divisions have been passed from one generation to the next into our current day. They have led to disparities in the life chances of a good portion of our population and made our entire country weaker for it.

Your alma mater, Bates College, was founded out of a desire to end these divisions, founded in the darkest hours before the Civil War by abolitionists who dreamed a world different than the one they had been born to, who welcomed the potential of people who did not look like themselves. And as you know, Bates was the first college in New England to admit women and one of the first to admit people of color. At Bates, you have proven that you can do well and do good at the same time.

"THE BROTHERHOOD OF MAN IN EVERY CONDITION."

When the Civil War broke out, half the freshman class volunteered to fight for the Union to abolish the sin of slavery, marching from Hathorn Hall to the railway station to the music of drum and fife.

And it was one of the earliest black graduates of Bates,

Thomas James Bollin, Class of 1879, who came up with a beautiful definition of equality that could be a standard for today. He said that social equality "is not equal rights before the law . . ." (of course, that is what he would have been seeking), "is not the equality of riches . . ." (which he would also have liked), "nor an equality in the simple right of franchise . . ." (which they were fighting for at that time). He said, no, "Social equality is the brotherhood of man in every condition."

I, too, would ask that we spend less time dwelling on what makes us different and more on what makes us so much the same, on our mutual commonality, what binds us together in our humanity, in our imperfections, in our Americanness, in our love and devotion, dreams and desires, the things that connect us all.

One of the great tragedies of the twentieth century was how our ancestors were pitted against one another. That millions of hopeful people arrived to our great cities from across the Atlantic, from across the Pacific, from across the Rio Grande and across the Mason-Dixon Line during the Great Migration.

These were all rural people far from their farms and hamlets trying to make a way for themselves in these big anonymous cities. They were our parents, our grandparents, our great-grandparents, and they were all the same people. Many had not been outside the counties into which they had been born. They all had the same

fears and the same courage, many of them fleeing perse-
cution, whether the pogroms of Europe or the lynchings
of Mississippi. But when they got here, they were divided
up based on what they looked like, the languages that
they spoke, the places which they had come from. Some
were permitted into unions, others were denied admit-
tance. Some could move where they wished. Others were
shut out by restrictive covenants and mob violence.

A TRUTH AND RECONCILIATION COMMISSION TO EXAMINE OUR HARD AND INTERWOVEN HISTORY.

We still live with the effects of these divisions to this day.
There is currently a debate raging in intellectual circles as
to whether we should study the idea of reparations for past
and continuing discriminations against the lowest-caste
people in our country. We don't know what will come of
it, or if there will be a study, but I am in favor of anything that gets us talking about what has gone unsaid for
so long. I truly believe that we need a truth and reconcilia-
tion commission to examine our hard and interwoven history so that we can heal and prosper as one. And it is my
hope, and I believe the hope of our country, that your generation finds a way finally to put an end to these divisions.

It will take courage to wrestle with the ghosts of the
past and the divisions of the present, the kind of courage

that I heard about from a colleague I once knew. A few years ago, I was having lunch with this colleague, a sandy-haired Midwesterner, who was senior to me and whom I did not know very well. We were talking about the wonders of teaching when the conversation took a sudden, unexpected turn. For some reason, he felt the need to share with me a deep tragedy within his family. Nearly all of the children in his family had been abused growing up.

The abuse had been so grave and had gone on for so long that it had torn the family apart. Relatives had stopped speaking to one another for decades.

"IT ENDS RIGHT HERE WITH ME."

The man told me that when he and his wife had their first child, he had to confront the darkness that had ruined the lives of so many children in his family. He looked into the crib at their beautiful and innocent newborn and held the baby close to his chest. He recalled the generations of abuse that had gone on before him. He was a good man, but in his veins coursed the blood of people who had done grievous things for generations. And he made a vow as he held that newborn. "It ends right here," he said. "It ends right here with me."

He ended up keeping that vow and having a close, loving, and fulfilling relationship with his now-grown children, a blessing denied the ancestors who had done so much harm. The abuses of the past had not been his fault or his doing, and the entire family had suffered for it. But he took it upon himself to be the one to end it. It takes courage to confront what has gone before you and more courage still to end an injustice and set a new course.

That is the choice before you and your generation. It may not be all that you do, but I hope that it will be one of the things that you will do on your journey. I hope that you will get to see the majesty of the Grand Canyon and the Serengeti, inhale the celestial scent of a Daphne, taste dim sum in Singapore, hear the mating call of a nightingale, create a better app for autocorrect—please!—and know true love.

No matter what course your life takes, there is but one thing that you absolutely must do before you leave this planet. You must make it a better place than it was before you got here. You must leave this world a better place than it would have been if you had not existed; fortunately or unfortunately, that is actually not as difficult a task as it sounds. Wars, poverty, inequality, intolerance, child abuse, climate change, sickness, disease, social injustice—there are so many challenges that we face, the world needs you now more than ever.

One of the most revered alumni to walk this campus was a man named Benjamin Elijah Mays, Class of 1920. He was living proof of how far you can go from where you stand today. He was the son of former slaves who became sharecroppers in South Carolina. His parents had not been taught to read and yet he journeyed to Bates for an education. He went on to get his Ph.D., become a renowned theologian, mentor to Dr. Martin Luther King Jr., and a college president. He had a beautiful way of describing the goal of life. He said: "To be able to stand the troubles of life, one must have a sense of mission and the belief that God sent him or her into the world for a purpose, to do something unique and distinctive, and that if he does not do it" (if he or she does not do it), "life will be worse off" (and I would add the world will be worse off) "because it was not done."

And as you go forth to make this world a better, fairer, more compassionate, kinder, and peaceful place, I hope that you will remember that you have the courage within you to do wondrous things, miracles even.

AGAINST DISCOURAGEMENT

Howard Zinn

SPELMAN COLLEGE, 2005

I AM DEEPLY HONORED to be invited back to Spelman after forty-two years.[*] I would like to thank the faculty and
trustees who voted to invite me, and especially your president, Dr. Beverly Tatum. And it is a special privilege to
be here with Diahann Carroll and Virginia Davis Floyd.

But this is your day—the students graduating today.
It's a happy day for you and your families. I know you

---

[*] In 1963, historian Howard Zinn was fired from Spelman College,
where he was chair of the history department, because of his civil
rights activities. In 2005, he was invited back to give the commencement address.

have your own hopes for the future, so it may be a little presumptuous for me to tell you what hopes I have for you, but they are exactly the same ones that I have for my grandchildren.

My first hope is that you will not be too discouraged by the way the world looks at this moment. It is easy to be discouraged, because our nation is at war—still another war, war after war—and our government seems determined to expand its empire even if it costs the lives of tens of thousands of human beings. There is poverty in this country, and homelessness, and people without health care, and crowded classrooms, but our government, which has trillions of dollars to spend, is spending its wealth on war. There are a billion people in Africa, Asia, Latin America, and the Middle East who need clean water and medicine to deal with malaria and tuberculosis and AIDS, but our government, which has thousands of nuclear weapons, is experimenting with even more deadly nuclear weapons. Yes, it is easy to be discouraged by all that.

But let me tell you why, in spite of what I have just described, you must not be discouraged.

I want to remind you that, fifty years ago, racial segregation here in the South was entrenched as tightly as was apartheid in South Africa. The national government, even with liberal presidents like Kennedy and Johnson in office, was looking the other way while black people were beaten and killed and denied the opportunity to vote. So black people in the South decided they had to do something by themselves. They boycotted and sat in and picketed and demonstrated, and were beaten and jailed, and some were killed, but their cries for freedom

My hope is that you will not be too discouraged by the way the world looks at this moment.

were soon heard all over the nation and around the world, and the president and Congress finally did what they had previously failed to do—enforce the Fourteenth and Fifteenth Amendments to the Constitution. Many people had said: the South will never change. But it did change. It changed because ordinary people organized and took risks and challenged the system and would not give up. That's when democracy came alive.

I want to remind you also that when the war in Vietnam was going on, and young Americans were dying and coming home paralyzed, and our government was bombing the villages of Vietnam—bombing schools and hospitals and killing ordinary people in huge numbers—it looked hopeless to try to stop the war. But just as in the Southern movement, people began to protest and soon it caught on. It was a national movement. Soldiers were coming back and denouncing the war, and young people were refusing to join the military, and the war had to end.

The lesson of that history is that you must not despair,

that if you are right, and you persist, things will change. The government may try to deceive the people, and the newspapers and television may do the same, but the truth has a way of coming out. The truth has a power greater than a hundred lies. I know you have practical things to do—to get jobs and get married and have children. You may become prosperous and be considered a success in the way our society defines success, by wealth and standing and prestige. But that is not enough for a good life.

Remember Tolstoy's story *The Death of Ivan Ilych*. A man on his deathbed reflects on his life, how he has done everything right, obeyed the rules, become a judge, married, had children, and is looked upon as a success. Yet, in his last hours, he wonders why he feels a failure. After becoming a famous novelist, Tolstoy himself had decided that this was not enough, that he must speak out against the treatment of the Russian peasants, that he must write against war and militarism.

My hope is that whatever you do to make a good life for yourself—whether you become a teacher, or social worker, or businessperson, or lawyer, or poet, or scientist—you will devote part of your life to making this a better world for your children, for all children. My hope is that your generation will demand an end to war, that your generation will do something that has not yet been done in history and wipe out the national boundaries that separate us from other human beings on this earth.

Recently I saw a photo on the front page of the *New York Times* which I cannot get out of my mind. It showed ordinary Americans sitting on chairs on the southern border of Arizona, facing Mexico. They were holding guns and they were looking for Mexicans who might be trying to cross the border into the United States. This was horrifying to me—the realization that, in this twenty-first century of what we call "civilization," we have carved up what we claim is one world into two hundred artificially created entities we call "nations" and are ready to kill anyone who crosses a boundary.

Is not nationalism—that devotion to a flag, an anthem, a boundary so fierce it leads to murder—one of the great evils of our time, along with racism, along with religious hatred? These ways of thinking, cultivated, nurtured, indoctrinated from childhood on, have been useful to those in power, deadly for those out of power.

Here in the United States, we are brought up to believe that our nation is different from others, an exception in the world, uniquely moral; that we expand into other lands in order to bring civilization, liberty, democracy. But if you know some history you know that's not true. If you know some history, you know we massacred Indians on this continent, invaded Mexico, sent armies into Cuba and the Philippines. We killed huge numbers of people, and we did not bring them democracy or liberty. We did not go into Vietnam to bring democracy; we did not invade Panama to stop the drug trade; we did not invade Afghanistan and Iraq to stop terrorism. Our aims were the aims of all the other empires of world history: more profit for corporations, more power for politicians.

The poets and artists among us seem to have a clearer understanding of the disease of nationalism. Perhaps the black poets especially are less enthralled with the virtues of American "liberty" and "democracy," their people having enjoyed so little of it. The great African American poet Langston Hughes addressed his country as follows:

> You really haven't been a virgin for so long.
> It's ludicrous to keep up the pretext . . .
> You've slept with all the big powers
> In military uniforms,
> And you've taken the sweet life
> Of all the little brown fellows . . .
> Being one of the world's big vampires,
> Why don't you come on out and say so
> Like Japan, and England, and France,
> And all the other nymphomaniacs of power . . .

I am a veteran of the Second World War. That was considered a "good war," but I have come to the conclusion that war solves no fundamental problems and only leads to more wars. War poisons the minds of soldiers, leads them to kill and torture, and poisons the soul of the nation.

Democracy does not come from the government, from on high; it comes from people getting together and struggling for justice.

My hope is that your generation will demand that your children be brought up in a world without war. If we want a world in which the people of all countries are brothers and sisters, if the children all over the world are considered as our children, then war—in which children are always the greatest casualties—cannot be accepted as a way of solving problems.

I was on the faculty of Spelman College for seven years, from 1956 to 1963. It was a heartwarming time, because the friends we made in those years have remained our friends all these years. My wife, Roslyn, and I and our two children lived on campus. Sometimes when we went into town, white people would ask: How is it to be living in the black community? It was hard to explain. But we knew this—in downtown Atlanta, we felt as if we were in alien territory, and when we came back to the Spelman campus, we felt that we were at home.

Those years at Spelman were the most exciting of my life, the most educational certainly. I learned more from my students than they learned from me. Those were the years of the great movement in the South against racial segregation, and I became involved in that in Atlanta; in Albany, Georgia; in Selma, Alabama; in Hattiesburg, Mississippi; and in Greenwood and Itta Bena and Jackson. I learned something about democracy: that it does not come from the government, from on high; it comes from people getting together and struggling for justice. I learned about race. I learned something that any intelligent person realizes at a certain point—that race is a manufactured thing, an artificial thing—and while race does matter (as Cornel West has written), it only matters because certain people want it to matter, just as nationalism is something artificial. I learned that what really matters is that all of us—of whatever so-called race and so-called nationality—are human beings and should cherish one another.

I was lucky to be at Spelman at a time when I could watch a marvelous transformation in my students, who were so polite, so quiet, and then suddenly they were leaving the campus and going into town, and sitting in, and being arrested, and then coming out of jail full of fire and rebellion. You can read all about that in Harry Lefever's book *Undaunted by the Fight*. One day Marian Wright (now Marian Wright Edelman), who was my student at Spelman and was one of the first arrested in the Atlanta sit-ins, came to our house on campus to show us a petition she was about to put on the bulletin board of her dormitory. The heading on the petition epitomized the transformation taking place at Spelman College. Marian had written [at the] top of the petition: "Young Ladies Who Can Picket, Please Sign Below."

My hope is that you will not be content just to be successful in the way that our society measures success; that you will not obey the rules, when the rules are unjust; that you will act out the courage that I know is in you. There are wonderful people, black and white, who are models. I don't mean African Americans like Condoleezza Rice, or Colin Powell, or Clarence Thomas, who have become servants of the rich and powerful. I mean W.E.B. DuBois and Martin Luther King Jr. and Malcolm X and Marian Wright Edelman and James Baldwin and Josephine Baker and good white folk, too, who defied the Establishment to work for peace and justice.

Another of my students at Spelman, Alice Walker, who, like Marian, has remained our friend all these years, came from a tenant farmer's family in Eatonton, Georgia, and became a famous writer. In one of her first published poems, she wrote:

It is true—
I've always loved
the daring
ones
Like the black young

man
Who tried
to crash
All barriers
at once,
wanted to
swim
At a white
beach (in Alabama)
Nude.

I am not suggesting you go that far, but you can help to break down barriers, of race certainly, but also of nationalism; that you do what you can—you don't have to do something heroic, just something—to join with millions of others who will just do something, because all of those somethings, at certain points in history, come together, and make the world better.

That marvelous African American writer Zora Neale Hurston, who wouldn't do what white people wanted her to do, who wouldn't do what black people wanted her to do, who insisted on being herself, said that her mother advised her: "Leap for the sun—you may not reach it, but at least you will get off the ground."

By being here today, you are already standing on your toes, ready to leap. My hope for you is a good life.

LISTEN TO YOUR MOTHER

Cecile Richards

BARNARD COLLEGE, 2014

A COUPLE OF DISCLAIMERS before I get started. First, in fact I myself didn't even walk in my graduation ceremony. I was otherwise occupied. At the time, students at Brown were protesting the university's investments in South Africa, and someone had to unfurl the banner from the second-floor window, so why not me? And it even partially paid off. Brown was in fact one of the first schools to divest, and it was an incredible honor to be back on campus not long ago when Dr. Ruth Simmons presented Nelson Mandela with an honorary degree from Brown.

And, second, I'm not a Barnard alum, though it seems like 90 percent of my colleagues at Planned Parenthood are. From our chief operating officer to our national board, Barnard alumnae are pretty much running the place. So thank you for that. It's a privilege to be here with all of you strong, beautiful, Barnard women today. You are in a pretty sweet position, because everyone from Tom Brokaw to Hillary Clinton is saying this is the century of the woman. And wow. Since we've had to wait 200,000 years—there's no time to waste!

Many of you may have already carefully plotted out your futures. Some of you have probably already written books and invented new apps and learned five languages—it's overwhelming. But if I may just speak for a moment to the other half of you who aren't totally certain what's next—let me just say: most of us never are. And as you begin the lifelong process of figuring it all out, I'll put in a plug for one option that your adviser may not have suggested.

Commencement speeches must have a message and so to make this simple, here's mine: *life as an activist, troublemaker, agitator is a tremendous option and one I highly recommend.*

In your four years at Barnard you've produced *The Vagina Monologues*, worked on mayoral and presidential campaigns, tutored kids in the neighborhood, taken back the night—and today you're getting ready to leave all that behind you and become a fully functioning adult with a real-life career. But all those amazing things, you've done here on campus. That could actually be your career—and lead to the most incredible life.

Life as an activist, troublemaker, agitator is a tremendous option and one I highly recommend.

We all need to acknowledge the privilege to which we were born, so here is mine: My parents were activists. Our dining room table wasn't where we ate—it was where we stuffed envelopes and sorted precinct lists for whatever campaign my folks were working on.

Growing up in Dallas in the sixties, my parents were into every movement that came through town. My dad defended conscientious objectors to the Vietnam War. My mother dragged us as kids to the grocery store, demanding to see the union label on the grapes. And then there was the day she went to hear an activist named Gloria Steinem and came home a new convert to this thing called women's liberation . . .

My first brush with the authorities was in seventh grade, the day I wore a black armband to school to protest the war—a heinous offense back in Texas. Being called to the principal's office at the tender age of thirteen sort of lit the fuse, but after surviving that standoff, I refused to take off my armband and that started my life of standing up for principles, even when they're controversial.

I know there's been some controversy about my appearance here today, and I appreciate the fact that Barnard women are the kinds of people who don't have to agree with someone to listen to her thoughts.

As you may know, Planned Parenthood was born in controversy—a tradition we've done our best to uphold for ninety-eight years. Nearly a century ago, Margaret Sanger opened the first—illegal—birth control clinic in the country, just down the road in Brooklyn. One day an undercover police officer posing as a mother showed up, busted Margaret, and threw her in jail—where she taught her fellow inmates about birth control!

And a movement was born. Ever since then we've had what you might call an affinity for challenging the status quo—something we share with Barnard. Barnard was founded 125 years ago, one of the first colleges in the world to embrace the radical idea that women deserve access to higher education. By the time the seventies and eighties rolled around, women had infiltrated just about every college campus in the country. We were no longer an exception. Suddenly we were a pretty hot commodity, and every school wanted women. One by one the seven sisters started coupling up with their co-ed counterparts—and all eyes turned to Barnard.

As Planned Parenthood board member and Barnard alum Anna Quindlen tells it, the conventional wisdom at the time was that Barnard should marry Columbia and take its name. But Barnard refused to fold. Fifty years ago the *New York Times* reported on Barnard's commencement, noting with pride how many graduates of the Class of 1964 were already married—they'd made

If you hold out for an invitation, chances are good you'll miss the party.

it! But the Class of 2014 is living up to your own definitions of success. A teacher who developed a history curriculum for high school students in Cape Town, South Africa. The captain of the Columbia women's lacrosse team. An entrepreneur who started an organization that sells jewelry while raising money and awareness around gun violence.

Educating and empowering women has turned out to be a growth industry, and Barnard was an early investor. But whether it's access to education or access to health care, women have only ever gotten what we fight for—nothing more and, I hope, nothing less.

We've been painfully reminded in the last few weeks that in too many parts of the world, women's education is still considered a radical idea—that girls can be shot at, kidnapped, even enslaved for having the audacity to go to school. Our fight is far from over. So thank you, Barnard, for more than a century of leading the charge. Working for social change, it is often hard to measure progress

when you're right in the middle of it. In fact, back when
my great-grandmother was a girl, the only folks who
couldn't vote under Texas law were "idiots, imbeciles,
the insane, and women." But wouldn't you know—just
two generations later, my mother, Ann Richards, was
elected governor.

That's the thing about women. Give us an inch and
we just won't quit. In the words of the legendary con-
gresswoman Bella Abzug: "Maybe we weren't at the
Last Supper, but we're certainly going to be at the next
one!" Take the more recent fight to pass the Affordable
Care Act. During an argument about women's health, a
male senator objected to insurance coverage for maternity benefits, saying he "wouldn't need them." Senator
Debbie Stabenow came right back without missing a beat
and said, "I bet your mother did." *For women, if we aren't
at the table, we are on the menu.* Having twenty women in
the U.S. Senate has changed the conversation on Capitol
Hill—though, as Senator Claire McCaskill says, you
know what would be better? Fifty.

And it's not just politics. All over the world, fearless
women are turning life as we know it upside down.

Take Ory Okolloh, who grew up in Nairobi, went to
college and law school in the States, and turned down
a job offer from a top firm in Washington to come home
after graduation for Kenya's 2007 election. When riots
broke out at the polls, Ory teamed up with a few friends

to create a crowdsourced map tracking incidences of violence in real time. They called it "ushahidi"—the Swahili word for testimony. Their platform is now used around the world, tracking everything from corruption by members of parliament to survivors of the hurricane in Haiti to traffic problems in Washington. And as for Ory—you can read all about her on *Time*'s list of the one hundred most influential people in the world.

Right here in New York, Reshma Saujani decided that if women were encouraged they could be superstars in the tech industry. She started "Girls Who Code," and chapters are now popping up all over the country, with young women learning the skills they need to take on careers in computer science.

And then there's Annie Clark and Andrea Pino, who met after they had each been sexually assaulted as students at the University of North Carolina and realized what happened to them was happening everywhere. And no one was talking about it. The first time they pitched their story to a national reporter, the reporter laughed. Two months later they were on the front page of the *New York Times*. That's when the floodgates opened. They heard from hundreds of survivors all over the country. And then this March, Annie and Andrea showed up at Senator Kirsten Gillibrand's office without an appointment and said, "Let's talk about ending sexual assault on campus." As Annie tells it: "We started talking—and she listened."

Today they've formed a national network of survivors, working with Congress and the White House to end campus sexual assault and demand justice.

The common theme? These women didn't wait to be asked. They just jumped headfirst. To borrow some wisdom from Lena Dunham: *"Don't wait around for someone else to tell your story. Do it yourself by whatever means necessary."* If you hold out for an invitation, chances are good you'll miss the party. And by the party I mean life.

Growing up, Mom always told me: The answer to life is yes. This is the only life you have so make the most of it. Take every opportunity and risk you can. You'll only regret the things you didn't do because you were afraid to try. Women often talk to me about a job and are worried they don't have the right degree. Or that they don't have all the right experience (I've never heard a man say any of that). Or that they want to have kids, and how's that going to work?

On that front, I was eight months pregnant with twins campaigning for my mother. You haven't lived until you've been on a float in the Yamboree parade in East Texas in a giant maternity dress—you can imagine. My true confession: Every single job I've interviewed for—from deputy chief of staff to Nancy Pelosi to running Planned Parenthood—I knew there was NO WAY I would get it. But frankly, I knew my mother would kill me if I didn't try. So I'm here to tell you—just do it. Whatever it is.

Say yes. You're Barnard women and certainly have the smarts and training to figure everything else out. As the late, great Nora Ephron advised, *"Be the heroine of your life, never the victim."*

And to all the parents: I know you're so proud of your daughters today—and trust me, if you think they're great as students, wait until you get to know them as fiercely independent adults. I've never cheered so loud as when my son Daniel became the vice chair of the women's rights group on his campus, where they finally got birth control for students! Or my daughter Hannah, who organized a rally in support of Planned Parenthood, complete with flash mob, at Wesleyan. And of course, there's the proud day when Rush Limbaugh came after my daughter Lily, right on the radio, for being an outspoken feminist! Now that's bragging rights. The Richards tradition— passed down through generations. My mom taught me so much. The basics: Never wear patterns on TV. If you're going to be in the public eye, you'll save yourself a lot of trouble if you pick a hairstyle and stick with it. Before naming your child, think about how it'll look on a bumper sticker.

But the most important lesson? There's one thing a life of activism offers that you can't get anywhere else: that's getting to do work that makes a difference. Mom said: "You may go somewhere else and you may make a lot of money, but you will never receive the kind of gratification that you receive from looking someone in the eye who says thank you for helping make my life better."

The world we live in can be tough. It can be unjust. But here's the great news: each of you has the power to do something about it. You get to build the world you want to live in.

It's not about being perfect, having it all, doing it all. It's about getting started. You've got work to do—so congratulations, and let's get to it.

Don't Wait to Change the World

Theodore M. Shaw

WESLEYAN UNIVERSITY, 2014

FIFTY YEARS AGO, IN this place, Dr. Martin Luther King Jr. received an honorary degree and delivered the baccalaureate sermon to the Wesleyan University Class of 1964. At thirty-five years old, he was more than halfway through his meteoric journey toward immortality. Less than a year earlier, he had delivered his now famous speech on the steps of the Lincoln Memorial. A few months later he would receive the Nobel Peace Prize. And yet, during this time, Dr. King passed through some of the most difficult days of his life. In September of 1963, a few weeks after the March on Washington, four little girls were murdered in the bombing of the Sixteenth Street Baptist Church in

Birmingham, Alabama. Two weeks after he spoke here on Denison Terrace, in Philadelphia, Mississippi, civil rights workers Michael Schwerner, James Chaney, and Andrew Goodman were abducted and murdered by local law enforcement officials and the KKK; a few weeks after that their bodies were found in an earthen dam. Only four years remained to his life. Unlike the image contemporary Americans have of Martin Luther King as the pied piper of nonviolent resistance, most people—even most African Americans—did not march with him. Nor was Martin Luther King Jr. THE leader of the civil rights movement. The movement was roiling and divided; King had many detractors within as well as outside of the civil rights movement.

In his few remaining years, Dr. King would turn to the issue of racial segregation in the North, to systemic issues of poverty and economic injustice, and to his opposition to the Vietnam War. He became persona non grata at the White House. When he spoke out against the war and against militarism, he was abandoned by many within the civil rights movement for not staying in his own lane. He did not live to complete his last crusade, against poverty and economic inequality, seemingly intractable problems, which continue to confront America today. At times, he struggled against depression. Yet, on that day, in this place, Martin Luther King Jr. spoke about faith, justice, and the hope for a better America.

King was not a stranger to Wesleyan. On several occasions he sought a brief refuge from the chaos and pressures of the civil rights movement, visiting his good friend

*O**ver the course of a long life, none of us gets it all right.***

Professor John Maguire, and connecting with David Swift, also of the religion department. They, and other members of the Wesleyan community, traveled south to march against segregation and racial injustice and for voting rights. But on that day, Martin Luther King promised that he would treasure his formal induction into the Wesleyan community. I like to think that Wesleyan can claim Dr. King. But even more important than that moment was what happened at Wesleyan after Dr. King's assassination. Although its "Vanguard Class" of African American students had arrived on campus in the fall of 1965, in the aftermath of post-assassination violence that set American cities afire, Wesleyan and other universities moved affirmatively and consciously to admit African American and other students of color. Wesleyan was on the front end of a wave of affirmative action that swept over colleges and universities across America.

In the days following Dr. King's assassination, Terence Cardinal Cooke, then archbishop of New York, sought a way to address the legacy of racial inequality. Unable to find a black priest to run it, he nonetheless sought to create a pool from which to draw African American candidates for the priesthood, and created a program called the Archbishop's Leadership Project. He found an Irish American priest in Harlem, Father John T. Meehan. To their credit, even after it became apparent that young black men from the tenements and housing projects of Harlem and the Bronx were interested in the civil rights and Black Power movements, and not the priesthood, Cardinal Cooke and Father Meehan continued the program with a redirected focus. On a splendid day, much like this, in the spring of 1972, Father Meehan brought me to Wesleyan. Neither one of us had ever been here before. I had applied late and blindly and had been wait-listed. After a brief stop at the admissions office, I wandered around the campus while Father Meehan visited with admissions officer Randy Miller, a name I doubt many people here would even know today. You cannot imagine how I fell in love with Wesleyan on that day, or the excitement I felt in the following days and weeks when I received my admission and financial aid notices. In the ensuing years, Father Meehan quietly stewarded scores of black students to Wesleyan and countless others to the best colleges and universities around the country. Celebrating his fiftieth anniversary in the priesthood this weekend, he is unable to be here in person, but Monsignor Meehan and I are always joined in spirit and in love, and it is he who deserves this honorary degree. I salute him today and every day. To be clear, what Cardinal Cooke and Monsignor Meehan practiced was affirmative action and it transformed countless lives in ways that will continue to echo across generations. Almost forty years later, many people, including some on the Supreme Court of the United States, have abandoned affirmative action and the term has become freighted with baggage. I am unapologetically, unashamedly, and unabashedly a beneficiary of affirmative action. If affirmative action meant shining the light of opportunity into places where it had not been shown before, in an effort to find capable and qualified students, I am a product of affirmative action.

In 1964, when Dr. King spoke here at Wesleyan, it was a monochromatic, single-sex institution, in which anyone other than straight, white males was either absent or an aberration. Change did not come accidentally, or even serendipitously. It came about as the consequence of deliberate, conscious decisions that were manifested in affirmative deeds.

Today we stand five years shy of the four hundredth anniversary of the involuntary arrival in Jamestown, Virginia, of the first of the people who would become African Americans. For three hundred and fifty of the three hundred and ninety-five years since then, until the end of the 1960s, black people in what is now the United States were subordinated by law, first in slavery, then in "Jim Crow" segregation. Stated differently, as we gather here today, nine out of every ten of the days of African Americans in colonial and post-independence America have been spent in slavery or legally imposed segregation and discrimination. I make this point not to belabor the tragedy and the long shadow of America's original sin, but to contextualize contemporary social, political, and legal discourse, which implausibly holds that the continuing and massive segregation and inequality that character-izes the lives of far too many Americans is unrelated to the events of those three hundred and fifty years. There are those who argue that we have graduated into a "post-racial" America, in which voluntary public school integra-tion efforts constitute racial discrimination; in which the protections of the Voting Rights Act are no longer neces-sary even as some states enact laws with the intention and/or effect of depriving some of the most vulnerable Americans of the sacred right to participate in democ-racy; in which racially disproportionate, massive overin-carceration of millions of people for nonviolent offenses is acceptable and even appropriate; and in which any and all conscious attempts to ameliorate racial inequality is itself deemed to be racial discrimination. Whether these arguments are proffered in good faith or whether they are intellectual dishonesty and arrogance masquerading as principle, I cannot discern. I simply know that, in spite of the tremendous progress we have made over the past fifty years, including the election of the first African American president, there is work to do if we are to continue the task of becoming "a more perfect union."

Choose hope in the face of every reason to give in to cynicism and despair.

Blindness is not my paradigm. Our goal must not be blindness, or the pretense that we do not see color, gender, or any other physical characteristic. The question is not whether we see race or color. Of course we do. The question is "what is its significance?" Having seen race or color or any other characteristic, is it a basis for subordination and discrimination? Or do we respect our differences and our diversity of backgrounds and experiences and work for racial justice? We must see all Americans, and all who live in America—indigenous, black, white, Latino, Asian American, immigrants, women, men, straight, gay, lesbian, transgendered, differentially abled, Christian, Jew, Muslim, Buddhist, Sikh, agnostic, atheist, wealthy, middle class, and poor—as part of Dr. King's "Beloved Community," and work to ensure equal treatment and a place for each of us. We need not shrink from difference. Differences need not divide us, if we respect commonalities, work for fairness and equity, and understand our diversity as strength, not as a weakness.

Even so, we live in a time of great divisions. Blue states and red states, Republicans and Democrats, progressives and conservatives, prolife and prochoice, gun control and gun rights advocates, people of faith and nonbelievers, and on and on. These divisions seem to grow greater every day. Increasingly, it seems that many of us demonize those with whom we disagree.

I want to urge something on each and every one of you who graduate today, whatever your politics may be. I have seen and read a number of reports in this graduation season that made me conscious of a newly endangered species, of which I have now become a member—the Commencement Speaker. I have lived my life as an advocate for racial, economic, and social justice. My politics are unapologetically progressive. As a student I demonstrated, and as a Wesleyan board member I advocated for divestment from companies that did business in South Africa. I have litigated in courts, advocated in legislatures, and argued in public discourse against cramped views and applications of civil and human rights. I have fought against injustice in every peaceful way I know how. I have debated and wrestled with my adversaries in any and all places where we could join issue. And it is important to continue to do so. Although sometimes heated, for the most part they have been healthy, necessary, and civil exchanges. I welcome these conversations and debates, for it would be a much less interesting world if we only spoke with or listened to people with whom we agree. Our views would be more dull and less developed if they were not sharpened and tested by challenge and disagreement. If we interacted only with those with whom we agree, our growth would be intellectually and socially stunted.

I believe that the views articulated by some in what is called the American Right, when they dare to characterize those with whom they disagree as not being "true Americans," are arrogant and dangerously misplaced. And I believe just as strongly that liberals and progressives err when we fail to calibrate carefully our opposition to the positions of our adversaries.

Moreover, I believe it is a mistake for any of us to hold those who enter into public service to rigid standards that condemn them to political and social exile when they take positions at odds with ours. Their words and deeds should not be beyond protest and criticism—even harsh criticism. But, for the most part, we must leave room for good-faith disagreement, growth, and redemption.

Last week we commemorated the sixtieth anniversary of *Brown v. Board of Education.* A unanimous Court under the leadership of Chief Justice Earl Warren decided *Brown*, one of the most important and revered decisions in American jurisprudence. In these days of bitter partisan division, nowhere more pronounced than on Supreme Court nominations, I have thought about the fact that Earl Warren, as attorney general of California during World War II, argued successfully for the internment of

Japanese American citizens who were loyal citizens. The civil rights/civil liberties community of today would have opposed Governor Warren's nomination to the Supreme Court, for good reason. And yet, the Warren Court was the most progressive in history. And *Brown* would not have been decided when and how it was without the leadership of Chief Justice Earl Warren.

Over the course of a long life, none of us gets it all right. We make mistakes. We hold views that evolve and change. We grow. We learn. The essence of liberalism is the open mind, tolerance, and a rejection of absolutism. I urge progressive voices not to mirror the intolerance of many on the Right.

Finally, it is customary to offer advice and wisdom to graduates. I have little to offer. I only observe that your generation, contrary to the "wisdom" of many in mine, is no less committed than was mine to making its mark on the world it is in the process of inheriting. Don't wait to change the world. Martin Luther King Jr. was twenty-six when he led the Montgomery bus boycott. In 1963, children, some as young as five years old, filled the jails of Birmingham, Alabama, protesting against segregation. Schoolchildren marched against apartheid in Soweto in the 1976 uprising. College and university students in the 1960s marched against the Vietnam War and for women's rights. Don't wait for the generation ahead of you to pass the baton to you if they do not willingly do so after they have run their leg of the race. The challenges presented by environmental sustainability, global warming, population growth, income and wealth inequality, racial and gender injustice, misogyny and child abuse, religious intolerance and ethnic hatred, war, totalitarianism and political oppression, and every other problem stemming from the human condition, are waiting for you. Take the baton. You won't solve them all, but make a dent. What better do you have to do with your lives than try? The genius of your generation has yet to be told. You are the first Internet Generation. There are cures for diseases and physical disabilities, some of which have plagued humanity from time immemorial, seemingly just around the corner. What will you do with and in your time?

In your personal life you will have triumphs and challenges, joys and sorrows, victories and defeats. When life shows you every reason to despair, don't do it. Humanity's greatest sins are the stepchildren of despair. Hope does not come serendipitously. It is a choice. Choose hope in the face of every reason to give in to cynicism and despair. The things that can sustain you in your life's journey have been taught to us, whatever our traditions are: faith, hope, and love. These are the things that illuminate our lives. The world is waiting. Go and get it. Life is shorter than you think. Don't wait. Grab the baton. Run your leg of the race, and pass it on. I have a friend who was imprisoned on Robbin Island with Nelson Mandela. Now the deputy chief justice on South Africa's Constitutional Court, Dikgang Moseneke is one of the most extraordinary people I know. During the days of transition from apartheid to majority rule, I heard him say, "If you want your dreams to come true, don't sleep."

A LEFT-HANDED
COMMENCEMENT ADDRESS

Ursula K. Le Guin

MILLS COLLEGE, 1983

I WANT TO THANK the Mills College Class of '83 for offering me a rare chance: to speak aloud in public in the
language of women.

I know there are men graduating, and I don't mean to
exclude them, far from it. There is a Greek tragedy where
the Greek says to the foreigner, "If you don't understand
Greek, please signify by nodding." Anyhow, commence-
ments are usually operated under the unspoken agreement that everybody graduating is either male or ought to
be. That's why we are all wearing these twelfth-century
dresses that look so great on men and make women look

either like a mushroom or a pregnant stork. Intellectual tradition is male. Public speaking is done in the public tongue, the national or tribal language; and the language of our tribe is the men's language. Of course women learn it. We're not dumb. If you can tell Margaret Thatcher from Ronald Reagan, or Indira Gandhi from General Somoza, by anything they say, tell me how. This is a man's world, so it talks a man's language. The words are all words of power. You've come a long way, baby, but no way is long enough. You can't even get there by selling yourself out: because there is theirs, not yours.

Maybe we've had enough words of power and talk about the battle of life. Maybe we need some words of weakness. Instead of saying now that I hope you will all go forth from this ivory tower of college into the Real World and forge a triumphant career or at least help your husband to and keep our country strong and be a success in everything—instead of talking about power, what if I talked like a woman right here in public? It won't sound right. It's going to sound terrible. What if I said what I hope for you is first, if—only if—you want kids, I hope you have them. Not hordes of them. A couple, enough. I hope they're beautiful. I hope you and they have enough to eat, and a place to be warm and clean in, and friends, and work you like doing. Well, is that what you went to college for? Is that all? What about success?

Success is somebody else's failure. Success is the American Dream we can keep dreaming because most people in most places, including 30 million of ourselves, live wide awake in the terrible reality of poverty. No, I do

What if I talked like a woman right here in public?

not wish you success. I don't even want to talk about it. I want to talk about failure.

Because you are human beings, you are going to meet failure. You are going to meet disappointment, injustice, betrayal, and irreparable loss. You will find you're weak where you thought yourself strong. You'll work for possessions and then find they possess you. You will find yourself—as I know you already have—in dark places, alone, and afraid.

What I hope for you, for all my sisters and daughters, brothers and sons, is that you will be able to live there, in the dark place. To live in the place that our rationalizing culture of success denies, calling it a place of exile, uninhabitable, foreign.

Well, we're already foreigners. Women as women are largely excluded from, alien to, the self-declared male norms of this society, where human beings are called Man, the only respectable god is male, the only direction is up. So that's their country; let's explore our own. I'm not talking about sex; that's a whole other universe, where every man and woman is on their own. I'm talking about society, the so-called man's world of institution-alized competition, aggression, violence, authority, and power. If we want to live as women, some separatism is forced upon us: Mills College is a wise embodiment of that separatism. The war-games world wasn't made by us or for us; we can't even breathe the air there without masks. And if you put the mask on you'll have a hard time getting it off. So how about going on doing things our own way, as to some extent you did here at Mills? Not for men and the male power hierarchy—that's their game. Not against men, either—that's still playing by their rules. But with any men who are with us: that's our game. Why should a free woman with a college education either fight Machoman or serve him? Why should she live her life on his terms?

Machoman is afraid of our terms, which are not all rational, positive, competitive, etc. And so he has taught us to despise and deny them. In our society, women have lived, and have been despised for living, the whole side of life that includes and takes responsibility for helpless-ness, weakness, and illness, for the irrational and the ir-reparable, for all that is obscure, passive, uncontrolled, animal, unclean—the valley of the shadow, the deep, the depths of life. All that the Warrior denies and refuses is left to us and the men who share it with us and there-fore, like us, can't play doctor, only nurse, can't be war-riors, only civilians, can't be chiefs, only Indians. Well, so that is our country. The night side of our country. If there is a day side to it, high sierras, prairies of bright grass, we only know pioneers' tales about it, we haven't got there yet. We're never going to get there by imitating Machoman. We are only going to get there by going our own way, by living there, by living through the night in our own country.

You will find you're weak where you thought yourself strong. You'll work for possessions and then find they possess you.

So what I hope for you is that you live there not as prisoners, ashamed of being women, consenting captives of a psychopathic social system, but as natives. That you will be at home there, keep house there, be your own mistress, with a room of your own. That you will do your work there, whatever you're good at, art or science or tech or running a company or sweeping under the beds, and when they tell you that it's second-class work because a woman is doing it, I hope you tell them to go to hell and, while they're going, to give you equal pay for equal time. I hope you live without the need to dominate, and without the need to be dominated. I hope you are never victims, but I hope you have no power over other people. And when you fail, and are defeated, and in pain, and in the dark, then I hope you will remember that darkness is your country, where you live, where no wars are fought and no wars are won, but where the future is. Our roots are in the dark; the earth is our country. Why did we look up for blessing—instead of around, and down? What hope we have lies there. Not in the sky full of orbiting spy-eyes and weaponry, but in the earth we have looked down upon. Not from above, but from below. Not in the light that blinds, but in the dark that nourishes, where human beings grow human souls.

CONTRIBUTORS

Chimamanda Ngozi Adichie is a Nigerian novelist and MacArthur Fellow (2008) whose work has been translated into thirty languages. Her books include *Purple Hibiscus*, which won the Commonwealth Writers' Prize and the Hurston/Wright Legacy Award; *Half of a Yellow Sun*, which won the Orange Prize, was a *New York Times* Notable Book, and a People and Black Issues Book Review Best Book of the Year; and *Americanah*, for which she won the National Book Critics Circle Award for Fiction.

Noam Chomsky is a world-renowned linguist, philosopher, cognitive scientist, and political activist. He is a professor of linguistics, emeritus, at the Massachusetts Institute of Technology and lectures widely on international affairs and U.S. foreign policy. He is the author of over one hundred books, including *Language and Mind*,

Manufacturing Consent, Profit Over People, Understanding Power, and *Rules and Representations.*

Marian Wright Edelman is an activist for the rights of children and has been an advocate for disadvantaged Americans her entire professional life. She was the first African American woman admitted to the Mississippi Bar. She practiced law with the NAACP Legal Defense and Educational Fund and her work included representing activists during the Mississippi Freedom Summer of 1964. After moving to Washington, D.C., she organized for the Poor People's Campaign of Martin Luther King Jr. and the Southern Christian Leadership Conference. In 1973 she founded the Children's Defense Fund, one of the nation's strongest voices for children and families, and remains its president today.

Paul Farmer is a medical anthropologist and physician who is well known for his humanitarian work providing health care for the world's poorest people. He is co-founder of the international social justice and health organization Partners In Health. He chairs the Department of Global Health and Social Medicine at Harvard Medical School and is the United Nations special adviser to the secretary-general on Community-Based Medicine and Lessons from Haiti.

Paul Hawken is an environmentalist, entrepreneur, and author. He has written several books, including four national bestsellers focused on business, activism, and sustainable practices. He has founded several companies, including one of the first natural food companies in the United States that relied only upon sustainable agricultural methods.

Barbara Kingsolver is a novelist, essayist, and poet. She has written over a dozen books including *Holding the Line: Women in the Great Arizona Mine Strike*, *The Poisonwood Bible* (a finalist for the Pulitzer Prize), and *Animal, Vegetable, Miracle*. Her work focuses on matters of social justice, biodiversity, and the interaction between humans and their communities and environments. In 2000 she was awarded the National Humanities Medal and in 2011 she won the Dayton Literary Peace Prize for the body of her work.

Tony Kushner is a playwright and screenwriter. His plays include *The Intelligent Homosexual's Guide to Capitalism and Socialism with a Key to the Scriptures* and *Angels in America*, for which he received the Pulitzer Prize for Drama and two Tony Awards. He wrote the screenplay for the 2012 film *Lincoln* for Steven Spielberg, he has translated and adapted plays by S. Ansky, Pierre Corneille, and Bertolt Brecht, and he wrote a children's opera with Maurice Sendak (on whom he has also written a monograph). In

2013 he received a National Medal of Arts for his work from President Barack Obama.

Ursula K. Le Guin is an author of novels, children's books, and short stories. Her work often depicts futuristic or imaginary alternative worlds in politics, the natural environment, gender, religion, sexuality, and ethnography. For her work she has received five Hugo Awards, five Nebula Awards, the Kafka Award, the PEN/Malamud Award, and three of her books have been finalists for the American Book Award and the Pulitzer Prize. Her 1973 novel *The Farthest Shore* won the National Book Award for Young People's Literature.

Wynton Marsalis is an internationally praised musician, composer, and educator, and is the artistic director of Jazz at Lincoln Center in New York City. The winner of nine Grammy Awards®, in 1983 he became the only artist ever to win Grammy Awards for both jazz and classical records—a distinction he earned again in 1984. He is the author of five books, including *Sweet Swing Blues on the Road* and *Moving to Higher Ground: How Jazz Can Change Your Life*.

Toni Morrison is an acclaimed novelist, editor, and professor whose works examine the struggles of the sexes; the races; and our communities. Her first novel, *The Bluest*

Eye, was published in 1970 when she was working at Random House acquiring and editing books by Muhammad Ali, Angela Davis, Gayl Jones, and Huey P. Newton. She went on to write such celebrated novels as *Song of Solomon*, *Sula*, *Jazz*, and *Tar Baby*. Her novel *Beloved* won the Pulitzer Prize for Fiction in 1988. In 1993 she became the first African American woman to win a Nobel Prize in Literature and in 2012 she was awarded the Presidential Medal of Freedom.

Martha Nussbaum is a philosopher and the Ernst Freund Distinguished Service Professor of Law and Ethics at the University of Chicago, a chair that encompasses appointments in the philosophy department and the law school. She is the author of numerous books, including *Not for Profit: Why Democracy Needs the Humanities* and *Political Emotions: Why Love Matters for Justice*.

Anna Quindlen is an award-winning writer and journalist. She was a columnist for the *New York Times* from 1981 to 1994. In 1992 her "Public and Private" column won the Pulitzer Prize for Commentary. From 2000 to 2009 she wrote the "Last Word" column for *Newsweek*. She is the author of six bestselling novels.

Cecile Richards is a leader in the field of women's health and reproductive rights. She is the president of the

Planned Parenthood Federation of America and in the
past has served as the deputy chief of staff for House
Democratic leader Nancy Pelosi.

Theodore M. Shaw is the Julius L. Chambers Distinguished Professor of Law and director of the Center for
Civil Rights at the University of North Carolina School
of Law at Chapel Hill. Previously, he was a professor
at Columbia University Law School and the University
of Michigan Law School, and also served as the fifth
director-counsel and president of the NAACP Legal
Defense Fund, the organization's legal arm founded by
Thurgood Marshall. He has litigated education, employment, voting rights, housing, police misconduct, capital
punishment, and other civil rights cases in trial and ap-
pellate courts, and in the United States Supreme Court.

Gloria Steinem is a feminist, journalist, and renowned
social and political activist. She became well known as a
leader in the women's liberation movement in the 1960s
and 1970s. Her 1969 article "After Black Power, Women's
Liberation" catapulted her to national fame as a feminist
leader. She was a columnist for *New York* magazine and a
co-founder of *Ms.* magazine.

Oliver Stone is a film director, screenwriter, producer,
and U.S. military veteran. He came to public prominence

between the mid-1980s and the early 1990s for writing and directing a series of films about the Vietnam War, in which he had participated as an infantry soldier. Many of Stone's films focus on contemporary and controversial American political and cultural issues during the late twentieth century. Stone has received three Academy Awards for his work on the films *Midnight Express*, *Platoon*, and *Born on the Fourth of July*.

Isabel Wilkerson is a journalist and author widely praised for her book *The Warmth of Other Suns: The Epic Story of America's Great Migration*. In 1994, while Chicago bureau chief of the *New York Times*, she became the first African American woman to win the Pulitzer Prize in journalism.

Howard Zinn (1922–2010) was a historian, author, playwright, and activist. He was a political science professor at Boston University for twenty-four years and prior to that taught history at Spelman College for seven years. In his lifetime Zinn wrote more than twenty books on civil rights, antiwar movements, and labor history, among them his bestselling *A People's History of the United States*.

PERMISSIONS

"Learn Not to Listen." Copyright © 2011 by Anna Quindlen, reprinted with permission courtesy of ICM Partners.

"Be In Time." Copyright © 2001 by Wynton Marsalis, reprinted with permission courtesy of the author.

"How to Be Hopeful." Copyright © 2008 by Barbara Kingsolver, reprinted with permission courtesy of The Frances Goldin Literary Agency.

"To All My Children." Copyright © 2008 by Marian Wright Edelman, reprinted with permission courtesy of the author.

"Who Will Defend the Earth?" Copyright © 2013 by Noam Chomsky, reprinted with permission courtesy of the author.

"The Pursuit of Meaningfulness." Copyright © 2011 by Toni Morrison, reprinted with permission courtesy of ICM Partners.

"Go the Distance." Copyright © 2007 by Gloria Steinem, reprinted with permission courtesy of the author.

"The World Is Waiting for You." Copyright © 2002 by Tony Kushner, reprinted with permission courtesy of the author.

"Allow Hope But Also Fear." Copyright © 2009 by Chimamanda

Adichie, reprinted with permission courtesy of The Wylie Agency LLC.

"On Empathy and Reason: Reporting a New Medical Discovery." Copyright © 2013 by Paul Farmer, reprinted with permission courtesy of the author.

"Not for Profit: Liberal Education and Democratic Citizenship." Copyright © 2009 by Martha Nussbaum, reprinted with permission courtesy of the author.

"Know Your History." Copyright © 2009 by Oliver Stone, reprinted with permission courtesy of the author.

"The Earth Is Hiring." Copyright © 2009 by Paul Hawken, reprinted with permission courtesy of the author.

"Make This World a Better Place." Copyright © 2014 by Isabel Wilkerson, reprinted with permission courtesy of the author.

"Against Discouragement." Copyright © 2005 by Howard Zinn, reprinted with permission courtesy of the Estate of Howard Zinn and the Howard Zinn Revocable Trust.

"Listen to Your Mother." Copyright © 2014 by Cecile Richards, reprinted with permission courtesy of the author.

"Don't Wait to Change the World." Copyright © 2014 by Theodore M. Shaw, reprinted with permission courtesy of the author.

"A Left-Handed Commencement Address." Copyright © 1983 by Ursula K. Le Guin, reprinted with permission courtesy of the author and Curtis Brown, LTD.

About the Editors

Tara Grove is the education editor at The New Press and a graduate of the University of Pennsylvania. **Isabel Ostrer** is a recent graduate of Harvard University, where she studied public health. They both went to college to figure out how they could make the world a more humane place to live. They currently live in New York City.

Publishing in the Public Interest

Thank you for reading this book published by The New Press. The New Press is a nonprofit, public interest publisher. New Press books and authors play a crucial role in sparking conversations about the key political and social issues of our day.

We hope you enjoyed this book and that you will stay in touch with The New Press. Here are a few ways to stay up to date with our books, events, and the issues we cover:

- Sign up at www.thenewpress.com/subscribe to receive updates on New Press authors and issues and to be notified about local events
- Like us on Facebook: www.facebook.com/newpressbooks
- Follow us on Twitter: www.twitter.com/thenewpress

Please consider buying New Press books for yourself; for friends and family; or to donate to schools, libraries, community centers, prison libraries, and other organizations involved with the issues our authors write about.

The New Press is a 501(c)(3) nonprofit organization. You can also support our work with a tax-deductible gift by visiting www.thenewpress.com/donate.

GUILDERLAND PUBLIC LIBRARY
2228 WESTERN AVENUE
GUILDERLAND, NY 12084
518-456-2400